W9-BRT-619

Nigeria

Nigeria

BY ANN HEINRICHS

Enchantment of the World™
Second Series

Children's Press®

An Imprint of Scholastic Inc.

NEW YORK   TORONTO   LONDON   AUCKLAND   SYDNEY
MEXICO CITY   NEW DELHI   HONG KONG
DANBURY, CONNECTICUT

Frontispiece: Niger River

Consultant: Patricia Agupusi, University of East Anglia, Norwich, United Kingdom

Please note: All statistics are as up-to-date as possible at the time of publication.

Book production by Herman Adler

Library of Congress Cataloging-in-Publication Data

Heinrichs, Ann.
  Nigeria / by Ann Heinrichs.
      p. cm. — (Enchantment of the world. Second series)
  Includes bibliographical references and index.
  ISBN-13: 978-0-531-20653-9
  ISBN-10: 0-531-20653-X
  1. Nigeria—Juvenile literature. I. Title. II. Series.
  DT515.22.H45 2010
  966.9—dc22   2009006655

1 2 3 4 5 6 7 8 9 10 R 19 18 17 16 15 14 13 12 11 10   62

Nigeria

Contents

Cover photo:
Nigerian woman

Lake Chad

Igbo pottery

Ancient Roots, Modern Challenges

ROOSTERS ARE CROWING AS MUYI WALKS THROUGH THE dusty streets of his village in Nigeria. Brightly dressed women glide by with baskets on their heads, bound for the weekly market. Dressed in his green school uniform, Muyi adjusts his backpack as he dodges the goats that cross his path. At last, he joins his fellow students as they exchange greetings with their teacher.

Opposite: **A dancer at a village festival in Nigeria wears an ornate costume.**

A man sells goats in a Nigerian market.

Ancient Roots, Modern Challenges **9**

Taking their seats in the crowded classroom, Muyi and the other students flash smiles as they pull green-and-white laptop computers out of their backpacks. Muyi takes notes on his laptop as the teacher lectures. He accesses the computer's built-in encyclopedia for a lesson on mammals' eyes. After school, he helps another student fix his broken keyboard.

Back in the home he shares with his grandmother, Muyi types his assignments on the laptop, stopping to look up words he doesn't understand. Muyi's name is short for Olumuyiwa.

A child sits in the doorway of his home on the outskirts of Abuja.

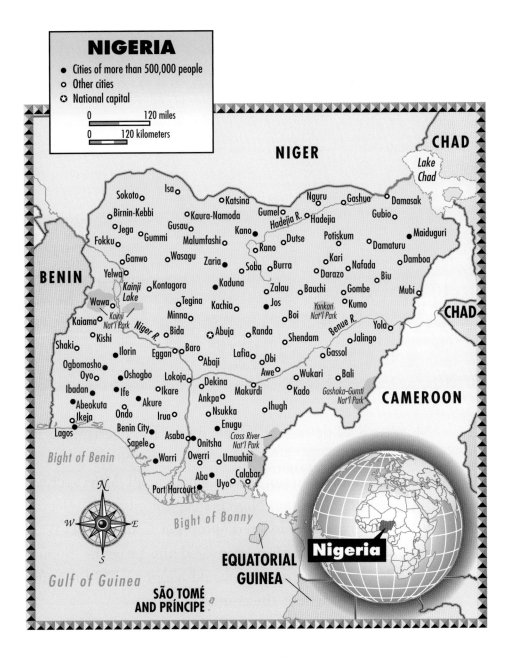

NIGERIA

- Cities of more than 500,000 people
- Other cities
- National capital

0   120 miles

0   120 kilometers

NIGER

CHAD

Lake Chad

Sokoto   Isa   Katsina   Nguru   Gashua   Damasak
Birnin-Kebbi   Kaura-Namoda   Gumel   Gubio
Jega   Gusau   Hadejia R.   Hadejia   Maiduguri
Fokku   Gummi   Malumfashi   Kano   Dutse   Potiskum   Damaturu
Ganwo   Wasagu   Zaria   Rano   Burra   Kari   Nafada   Damboa
Yelwa   Soba   Darazo   Biu
Kainji   Kontagora   Kaduna   Zalau   Bauchi   Gombe   Mubi
Wawa   Lake   Tegina   Kachia   Jos   Yankari   Kumo
Kaiama   Minna   Boi   Nat'l Park
Kainji   Niger R.   Bida   Abuja   Randa   Benue R.   Yola
Nat'l Park
Shaki   Kishi   Baro   Shendam   Jalingo
Ilorin   Eggan   Lafia   Obi   Gassol
Ogbomosho   Oshogbo   Abaji   Awe   Wukari   Bali
Oyo   Lokoja   Dekina   Kado   Gashaka-Gumti
Ibadan   Ife   Ikare   Ankpa   Ihugh   Nat'l Park
Abeokuta   Akure   Irua   Nsukka
Ikeja   Ondo   Enugu
Lagos   Benin City   Asaba   Cross River
Sapele   Onitsha   Nat'l Park
Warri   Owerri   Umuahia
Aba   Calabar
Port Harcourt   Uyo

BENIN

CHAD

CAMEROON

Bight of Benin

N
W   E
S

Bight of Bonny

Gulf of Guinea

SÃO TOMÉ
AND PRÍNCIPE

EQUATORIAL
GUINEA

Nigeria

In his native Yoruba language, it means "God has brought this one." Muyi was named for being a gift from God, and he feels that his educational opportunity is also a precious gift.

The Market in Sokoto in 1853, by Eberhard Emminger. Sokoto has long been an important center of Islamic learning in Nigeria.

Muyi's school day is not a typical one. In Nigeria, Africa's most populous country, few students have computers. Millions of Nigerian children do not attend school at all. Muyi's school on the outskirts of Abuja, Nigeria's capital city, was selected for a test program called One Laptop per Child (OLPC). A U.S. nonprofit organization sponsored the program, hoping that the Nigerian government would adopt OLPC for many more schools throughout the country.

Muyi is growing up in a country with a history of glory and struggle. Ancient kingdoms once flourished across Nigeria, where diverse ethnic groups excelled in government, trade, and the arts. Traditional ways of life were destined to change when Europeans reached Nigeria's shores. The Europeans began shipping out people for the slave trade. Eventually, millions of people would be kidnapped and sold abroad.

After decades as a British colony, Nigeria won its independence in 1960. Still, the bright promises of freedom remained beyond reach. The country was soon embroiled in a series of military dictatorships and corrupt governments, and a bloody civil war. Meanwhile, with its rich oil reserves, Nigeria became one of the wealthiest oil-producing nations in the world. While the country was focused on oil, however, matters such as roads and education were neglected.

A Nigerian family relaxes at home.

Now that Nigeria has a democratic government, national priorities are shifting. Though the nation has many promising plans, they sometimes meet political, legal, technical, and financial obstacles. In Muyi's world, this state of affairs has had a personal impact: the government canceled the laptop venture, and the laptops were taken away. But Muyi's computer skills may prove to be useful one day, as this land of ancient roots struggles to meet 21st-century challenges.

A Varied Land

Many kinds of plants grow in Nigeria's lush rain forests.

NIGERIA'S DIVERSE LANDSCAPE COVERS A VAST EXPANSE of West Africa. It stretches from the broad grasslands and arid semidesert of the north, to the spectacular rock formations of the interior, and the dense swamps and tropical rain forests of its southern coast.

Nigeria is the 14th-largest country among Africa's 53 nations and the 32nd-largest country in the world. It covers 356,669 square miles (923,768 square kilometers). That's about the size of Texas and Minnesota combined.

Opposite: **Tall rock formations dot the landscape of central Nigeria.**

A Varied Land   **15**

Lake Chad is a large, shallow lake. Its size changes dramatically depending on rainfall and how much of its water is used for irrigation.

Nigeria is located in West Africa, the great bulge on the western part of the African continent. It lies on West Africa's southern coast, facing the Gulf of Guinea, an arm of the Atlantic Ocean. Nigeria's southern tip is only about 300 miles (480 km) north of the equator. Four other countries border Nigeria. To the west is Benin, and to the east, across a string of mountain ranges, is Cameroon. Niger lies to the north, and Chad borders a small part of northeastern Nigeria across Lake Chad.

The Niger River, the Delta, and the Coastal Plains

Nigeria gets its name from the great Niger River, the major river in Nigeria and in all of West Africa. The Niger is Africa's third-longest river, after the Nile and the Congo. It forms the Niger-Benin border before entering western Nigeria. The Niger's largest tributary, the Benue River, enters Nigeria from Cameroon, to the east. It joins the Niger in central Nigeria. The Niger River then continues south to the Gulf of Guinea. Looking at Nigeria from the sky, the Benue and Niger rivers form a distinct Y shape.

The Niger River serves as an important transportation route for people in Nigeria.

Looking at Nigeria's Cities

Lagos (below), Nigeria's largest city, was first settled by Yoruba people in the 1400s. Then it became a trading post between Nigeria's Benin Kingdom and the Portuguese until the British took it over in the 1800s. From 1914 to 1991, Lagos was Nigeria's capital city. The heart of the city is Lagos Island, or Eko, southwest of the Niger Delta. This island is the business and market center. Sitting majestically on the island is the Oba's Palace, home of Lagos's traditional ruler. Parts of the palace are more than 200 years old. Other attractions are the National Museum, the National Theatre, and the Central Mosque. Nearby Victoria Island is mainly a residential area, with beautiful homes and gardens as well as shopping districts and popular beaches. Most of Lagos's population, however, lives on the mainland, where many industries and entertainment centers are located.

Ibadan, the second-largest city, is located near a thickly wooded forest in southwestern Nigeria. Its notable sites include Cocoa House, the first skyscraper in Africa, along with the huge Dugbe Market and the University of Ibadan. The city is the starting point for visits to nearby historic towns such as Oyo and Ife.

Kano, in northern Nigeria, is the nation's third-largest city. More than 1,000 years old, it served as a bustling center for trade between the Sahara, a vast desert to the north, and lands to the south. Today, it is a major trade, transportation, and communications hub for West Africa. Major sites in Kano include the Gidan Rumfa, or Emir's Palace, a stone-walled complex dating from the 1400s. The Gidan Makama Museum highlights the history of Kano and of the region's Hausa-Fulani people. Kano's Central Mosque is one of the largest in Nigeria, and its minarets (towers) offer a spectacular view of the city below.

Once the seat of the Benin Kingdom, Benin City is steeped in history. From the 1400s through the 1600s, the powerful *oba* (king) of Benin ruled over a large army and a diverse economy. Benin artisans of the time produced exquisite brass sculptures, some of which are on display at the city's museum. Today, Benin City is the center of Nigeria's rubber industry. Historic landmarks include Chief Ogiamen's House, built in the 1100s, and a moat built around the city for defense in the 1200s.

Near the mouth of the Niger River, the waters fan out into a maze of streams that empty into the gulf. Here, the coast is jagged, with many lagoons, or little bays, reaching inland. This swampy, low-lying region is called the Niger Delta. The delta is the most oil-rich region of the country and is the hub of the nation's highly profitable oil industry.

To the east and west of the delta are coastal plains marked by swamps, lagoons, and thick forests. Southwest of the delta is Lagos, Nigeria's largest city and major port. It occupies several islands as well as part of the mainland.

A man catches fish in a pond in the Niger Delta. This region is filled with wetlands.

The Highlands

The most mountainous part of the country is eastern Nigeria, along the Cameroon border. The eastern highlands

Nigeria's Geographic Features

Area: 356,669 square miles (923,768 sq km)

Greatest Distance North to South: About 650 miles (1,045 km)

Greatest Distance East to West: About 750 miles (1,200 km)

Highest Elevation: Chappal Waddi, 7,936 feet (2,419 m) above sea level

Lowest Elevation: Sea level, at the Atlantic Ocean

Coastline: 530 miles (853 km)

Longest River: Niger River

Average High Temperatures: In Lagos, 90°F (32°C) in March and 82°F (28°C) in September; in Kano, 99°F (37°C) in March and 88°F (31°C) in September

Average Low Temperatures: In Lagos, 79°F (26°C) in March and 55°F (13°C) in September; in Kano, 66°F (19°C) in March and 70°F (21°C) in September

Average Annual Rainfall: In Lagos, 72 inches (183 cm); in Kano, 33 inches (84 cm)

are made up of several mountain ranges, including the Mandara, Shebshi, Alantika, Gotel, and Mambila mountains. Nigeria's highest peak, Chappal Waddi, rises to 7,936 feet (2,419 meters) in the Gotel Mountains. The Nigeria-Cameroon border crosses through its summit. The highest point wholly within Nigeria is Dimlang Peak, rising 6,699 feet (2,042 m) in the Shebshi Mountains.

The western highlands, in west-central Nigeria, are known as the Yoruba Highlands or the Plateau of Yorubaland. They are named for the Yoruba people, whose traditional homeland is here. This rugged area is marked by dome-shaped granite hills.

The Jos Plateau is in central Nigeria, north of where the Niger and the Benue rivers meet. It rises steeply above the surrounding plains. This is Africa's major tin-mining region. Many rivers rise on the plateau and flow southward into the Niger and the Benue. Some of them form beautiful waterfalls as they cascade down the plateau's slopes.

The Jos Plateau is a mixture of grasslands and small forests along rivers.

The Northern Plains

High, grassy plains called savannas cover northern Nigeria. Here and there, rock formations jut up from the plains. North of Nigeria, these dry grasslands reach the rim of the Sahara. The northern plains are often called the Plains of Hausaland, after its Hausa residents. The Gongola, Sokoto, Kaduna, and

Camels munch on leaves in the dry savanna of northern Nigeria.

High waters flood a village in Nigeria.

other rivers flow through these plains on their way to the Niger River. They form many waterfalls along their courses. In the drier areas of the northern savanna, drought and overgrazing have drastically reduced the grass cover, causing the soil to dry and lose valuable nutrients through wind and water erosion.

In the northeast, the plains slope down to the Lake Chad basin. Short grasses and scattered trees grow in its sandy soil. This region becomes swampy during the rainy season, but lack of rain often causes serious droughts. Nigeria's northwest corner is the low-lying Sokoto Plain. Floodwaters gather here during the rainy season, leaving fertile mineral deposits behind but sometimes causing devastating floods.

A Varied Land **23**

During the heat of the day, people seek out shade, where they find some relief from the intense sunlight.

Climate

Temperatures across Nigeria are warm to hot, without extreme variations throughout the day or the year. On a countrywide basis, Nigeria's year-round temperatures average from 77 to 82 degrees Fahrenheit (25 to 28 degrees Celsius). In general, the north is hot and dry, and the middle belt has a warm, moist climate. Southern Nigeria is hot and wet year-round.

Nigeria has two basic seasons—rainy and dry. Warm, moist air blowing in from the Atlantic Ocean brings rains and high humidity. The length of the rainy season varies from north to south. In the country's middle belt, the rains last from April or May through September or October. In the Niger Delta region to the south, rains last virtually all year, with annual rainfall reaching more than 160 inches (400 centimeters). The far north receives only about 20 inches (51 cm) of rain each year.

The dry season begins with the *harmattan*, a northeasterly wind blowing from the Arabian Peninsula across the Sahara. It creates a dusty, hazy atmosphere and brings cool, dry temperatures that last until February. The latter part of the dry season, February through March, is the hottest time of the year in much of Nigeria, with temperatures reaching 90 to 100°F (32 to 38°C) or more. The northern third of the country suffers the hottest, driest conditions. Maiduguri, in the northeast, often has temperatures over 100°F (38°C) in April and May. Occasional droughts can destroy crops and diminish the water supply in this region.

During dry periods, brush-fires are a common danger.

From Swamp to Savanna

Drill monkeys live only in the forests of southeastern Nigeria and nearby regions.

Elephants, lions, crocodiles, and monkeys are just a few of Nigeria's spectacular wildlife species. These creatures require a variety of habitats, and they survive because of Nigeria's diverse climate and vegetation.

Plant life in Nigeria generally matches the amount of rainfall in a given area. Savanna grasslands cover the drier northern half of the country, and forests dominate in the wetter southern half. Both the savannas and the forests have varying types of vegetation, running in horizontal bands across the country. Let's look at each type, moving from south to north. Then we'll explore the animals that make their homes there.

Opposite: **Elephants are the largest land animals in the world. Some stand 13 feet (4 m) at the shoulder.**

Thick mangrove swamps provide a hiding place for boats filled with stolen oil.

Swamps

Forests cover only about 12 percent of Nigeria's land area. The three types of forestland found in the country are saltwater swamp, freshwater swamp, and tropical rain forest.

Along the coast and in the Niger Delta, waves of salty seawater wash inland, mixing with freshwater from rivers emptying into the sea. This creates brackish water, a mixture of salt water and freshwater. Brackish beaches, lagoons, and creeks are lined with several species of mangrove trees. Unlike most trees, mangroves can grow in salty water. Mangrove swamps are valuable because they protect coastlines from storms and heavy waves, and their tall roots provide a safe habitat for fish and other water creatures.

Nigeria has the largest concentration of mangroves in Africa and the fourth-largest in the world. But over the years, oil leaks and spills, logging for firewood, and clearing for human settlements have destroyed much of the mangroves. The Mangrove Forest Conservation Society of Nigeria (MFCSN) and the Green Movement, a Nigerian environmental and human rights organization, are working with local communities to preserve the mangroves and pressuring the government to establish protected mangrove reserves.

Farther inland, beyond the reach of seawater, lie freshwater swamps. They cover much of the upper Niger Delta. Raffia palms are the most common vegetation here. People use raffia leaf fibers for weaving mats, baskets, ropes, and other items.

A Nigerian woman weaves a mat. Traditionally, people have used raffia palms for weaving.

Oil palm trees produce large clusters of fruit. The fruit contains soft pulp that is used to make palm oil.

North of the swamps is a wide belt of tropical rain forest. It receives plenty of rainfall, so it supports a great diversity of plant life. The rain forest grows in three layers, or stories. The lowest level consists of grasses and shrubs. Hundreds of tree species make up the dense middle story, growing 60 to 80 feet (18 to 24 m) high. Oil palm trees are among the most valuable species. They are a source of cooking oil and soap, and their oil is also made into a sweet wine. Large hardwood trees such as *iroko*, which is used as a building material, also grow in the middle section. A few scattered species that grow as high as 100 to 200 feet (30 to 60 m) make up the upper story. They include mahogany, tropical cedar, and *obeche*, which is often used to build saunas (bathhouses) because it doesn't splinter.

Deforestation: A National Epidemic

Deforestation is one of Nigeria's worst environmental problems. Between 1990 and 2005, the country lost 35.7 percent of its forest cover. According to the Food and Agriculture Organization (FAO), a United Nations agency devoted to improving farming and forestry worldwide, Nigeria had the seventh-largest forest loss in the world during the period from 2000 to 2005.

Many different human activities are contributing to the destruction of the forests. Farmers burn them off to create more farmland, and these fires sometimes burn out of control. Agricultural companies and oil companies clear trees to make way for plantations and roads. Commercial loggers cut down tropical forest trees for sale, and other people cut trees for firewood. More trees are cleared for road building and oil drilling. As a result, Nigeria's tropical forests are disappearing at an alarming rate. Forest reserves are the only places where these forests are expected to survive in the future. Still, some people continue to settle and work in protected areas.

Much of Nigeria's rain forest has been cleared to make way for species that generate income. Plantations grow citrus fruit, oil palm, cocoa, rubber, and many other valuable trees. Some plantations produce crops such as cassava, a root crop that is the basis of the Nigerian diet. Secondary forest, or second-growth forest, is the vegetation that grows in areas where the original trees have been cleared. In Nigeria, much of the secondary forest consists of oil palm trees, either planted deliberately or left to fill in naturally.

Tamarind trees produce large pods that hold hard seeds amid a thick pulp. The pulp is a tasty treat, both sweet and sour.

Savannas

Just north of the rain forest, Nigeria's savannas begin. From south to north, the three types of savanna are Guinea savanna, Sudan savanna, and Sahel savanna. These grasslands, especially the Guinea and the Sudan savannas, are Nigeria's major regions for growing grains, grasses, vegetables, and cotton.

Tall grasses and trees grow in the moist Guinea savanna. Trees tend to gather in clusters here, rarely rising over 20 feet (6 m). Common species include baobab trees; tamarind trees, which produce a spicy fruit; and locust bean and oil bean trees, whose seeds are used in cooking. In between the trees is elephant grass, which often reaches 10 feet (3 m) tall. It's a favorite food for elephants. The Guinea savanna is rapidly expanding southward as more and more rain forest is burned off or cut down.

Shorter grasses grow in the drier Sudan savanna. Here, the trees are shorter, too, and spaced farther apart. These species tolerate drought well. They include acacia, tamarind, doum palm, and baobab. Along the rivers are gallery forests, or narrow strips of forest that get moisture from the rivers.

Some parts of the northern savanna are densely populated, especially around large cities such as Kano, Katsina, and Sokoto. Residents have removed much of the vegetation through burning, farming, and grazing. In some parts of the far north, the vegetation has been almost totally stripped. With nothing to hold fertile soil in place, winds blow it away and sweep the sands of the Sahara into Nigeria.

Nigeria's northeast corner lies in the Sahel savanna, a very dry, semidesert region. Short grasses grow in clumps here, with stretches of sandy soil between them. Most of the widely spaced trees in this region are acacias.

The National Flower

Nigeria's national flower is *Costus spectabilis*, or the spectacular costus. Commonly seen across the savanna, this wildflower has a brilliant, broad-petaled yellow blossom. Some people use the plant for medicinal purposes, applying the leaves to skin irritations or chewing them as a remedy for fever. *Costus spectabilis* is featured on Nigeria's national coat of arms.

Nigeria is home to an amazing variety of wild animals. Unfortunately, many native species are disappearing from the forests and grasslands as human settlement expands and farming, logging, and other industries destroy habitat. Animals are safest in Nigeria's national parks, game and forest reserves, and private wildlife protection areas.

Both forest and savanna animals roam through the vast Gashaka-Gumti National Park in eastern Nigeria. Cross River National Park, in the far southeast, is a rich rain

A saddle-billed stork holds a fish in its bill. This is one of the many bird species that lives at Yankari National Park.

Gashaka-Gumti National Park

Gashaka-Gumti is Nigeria's largest national park. This natural wilderness covers more than 2,600 square miles (6,700 sq km) in the mountainous east, alongside the Cameroon border. The park's rugged terrain ranges from steep, rocky slopes and luxuriant mountain rain forests to deep valleys, savanna woodlands, and swamps. At the southern end of the park rises Chappal Waddi, Nigeria's highest peak. Leopards, golden cats, monkeys, and giant forest hogs are some of the park's rain forest inhabitants. Across the savannas roam wild species such as buffalo, lions, elephants, wild dogs, and various antelope.

forest habitat. Kainji National Park, in western Nigeria, surrounds Kainji Lake, an artificial lake created by a dam on the Niger River. It preserves vast savanna woodlands. Yankari National Park, near Bauchi in northeast-central Nigeria, is one of the country's largest, most popular game reserves. Visitors from around the world come to this savanna woodland to see its large elephant herd as well as hundreds of species of migrating birds. These are just a few of Nigeria's spectacular wildlife sanctuaries.

Creatures of the Forests and Savannas

Elephants and buffalo are among Nigeria's largest mammals. They inhabit both forests and grasslands, feeding on leaves and grass. Lions take cover in tall grasses, stalking prey such as antelope. Leopards and cheetahs are common predators, too, as are jackals and spotted hyenas.

About two dozen species of antelope graze across the savanna. Some of the larger species are hartebeests, waterbucks, bushbucks, roan antelope, and giant elands. Oribi are graceful, slender antelope that can run up to 30 miles per hour (48 kph).

A mongoose holds an egg. Mongooses also eat lizards, snakes, rodents, and other creatures.

Little deer called duikers roam the forests, along with small carnivores, or meat eaters, such as mongooses and civets. Pangolins are scaly anteaters that inhabit the forests, sleeping by day and feeding on insects at night. They are endangered in Nigeria because people hunt them for food.

Nigeria's giant forest hog is the largest pig species in the world. Adults measure about 35 inches (89 cm) at the shoulder and weigh about 225 pounds (102 kilograms). These stocky black hogs have giant wartlike growths beneath their eyes, a long snout, and tusks. They spend time in both the forests and the savannas, often wallowing in water or mud.

Apes and Monkeys

Several species of apes and monkeys live in Nigeria. A small population of gorillas lives in the rugged, mountainous regions of the east. Cross River gorillas, classified as critically endangered, are the rarest gorillas in the world. Their numbers have been cut down by hunting, and fewer than 300 individuals remain. They are protected in the Afi and Mbe mountain wildlife sanctuaries and Cross River National Park.

Gorillas have five long toes on each foot. They can grasp objects with their hands and their feet.

Tails or No Tails?

Scientists classify apes and monkeys as higher primates—a group that includes humans. What's the difference between apes and monkeys? Apes are usually larger than monkeys, and they have no tails. Many ape species have arms that are longer than their legs. Gorillas, chimpanzees, and orangutans are apes. Monkeys usually have tails, and their arms are shorter than their legs or the same length. Monkeys include baboons, macaques, and many long-tailed monkeys of Africa, Asia, and Central and South America.

Chimpanzees—which are apes, not monkeys—have become extinct in some African countries as a result of hunting and deforestation. In Nigeria, chimps survive in protected areas such as Gashaka-Gumti National Park. There, high in the trees, they build nests of twigs and leaves where they can take naps and sleep at night. By day, they swing from branch to branch and forage for insects and fruit.

A mother chimpanzee holds an infant. A young chimp stays with its mother until about age seven.

Many monkey species inhabit the rain forests and mixed forest areas. Some can be identified by sight, but others are more likely to be heard. Black-and-white colobus monkeys swish bushy white tails, and putty-nosed guenons have a bright nose on their black face. Mona monkeys make a deep, booming call, and olive baboons roar, bark, and grunt.

Black-and-white colobus monkeys have fringes of long white fur that fall from their shoulders. Most of their diet consists of leaves.

Endangered monkeys inhabiting Nigeria include the red-bellied monkey, the drill, and Sclater's guenon, which lives only in Nigeria. Drills are short-tailed baboons found in the tropical rain forest, where they live on a diet of fruit, seeds, roots, insects, and small animals.

Many organizations are working to protect Nigeria's monkeys and apes. One is the Gashaka Primate Project, whose members study the animals' feeding, communication, and reproduction habits in Gashaka-Gumti National Park in order to create the best environment for survival. The Centre for Education, Research and Conservation of Primates and Nature is a forest monkey rehabilitation center in Calabar, southeastern Nigeria. It rescues injured monkeys, cares for them, and releases them back into the wild. The Pandrillus Drill Rehabilitation and Breeding Center, also in Calabar, rescues and breeds drills in hopes of saving them from extinction.

Crocodiles lurk in the shallows at the edges of lakes and rivers. They attack their prey when it comes to drink from the water.

Wetland Creatures

Crocodiles, hippopotamuses, manatees, turtles, tortoises, toads, frogs, and a variety of water snakes live in wetlands, rivers, and lakes. Waterbirds such as herons, fish eagles, kingfishers, and darters feed on fish. Some of the fish-eating mammals are marsh mongooses, civets, genets, and otters. All are excellent swimmers. Common fish in Nigeria's inland lakes and streams are catfish, tilapia, and Nile perch. The Atlantic coastal region has abundant shad and shellfish such as shrimp.

Two kinds of hippopotamuses live in Nigeria. The African giant hippopotamus stays around rivers and lakes in the savanna. The much smaller pygmy hippopotamus inhabits the Niger Delta.

The National Bird

The black-crowned crane is the national bird of Nigeria. This graceful, long-legged bird has a slate-gray body, a black forehead and crown, red-and-white cheek patches, and a spray of stiff, golden feathers on top of its head. Although black-crowned cranes were once common in Nigeria's grasslands and swamps, only a few of them survive there today. Land development and drought have damaged their habitat, and they have also been hunted for food and trapped for sale.

Bush Meat and Poaching

In most rural communities, the main source of protein in people's diets is wild animal meat, known as bush meat. Residents hunt the edible animals in their area. Procuring bush meat to eat at home and selling bush meat in the market are common practices. Unfortunately, hunters do not typically distinguish between common animals and endangered animals.

Poaching—or illegal hunting and trapping—is a serious threat to many wildlife species. Many poachers ship live animals overseas, where collectors pay high prices for rare or unusual species. The animals are often packed in wooden crates and smuggled out through international airports. Although such animal exports are against the law, airport officials routinely overlook the practice, and the government is lax in enforcing the laws.

Some poachers target animals such as gorillas, chimpanzees, drill monkeys, and giant tortoises and ship them to overseas zoos. Others trap birds that are in high demand as pets. For example, the African grey parrot, a grey bird with a scarlet tail, sells for several hundred dollars in the United States and Europe. Poachers may ship out dozens or even hundreds of them in one batch.

Birds and other small animals typically do not tolerate these shipments well because of the shortage of air and food and the stress of jostling around in the crates. Many die before they reach their destinations. Still, profits from the surviving animals are high enough to keep the poachers in business.

The Long Road to Nationhood

NIGERIA'S EARLIEST KNOWN RESIDENTS LIVED AT IWO Eleru, a site near Akure in what is now the southwestern part of the country. Stone tools and human remains found there date from as early as 9000 BCE. People may have lived even earlier at Ugwuelle-Uturu, near Okigwe in the southeast. Nigeria's most advanced prehistoric culture, however, was the Nok civilization. It flourished in the Jos Plateau region from about 500 BCE to 200 CE. The Nok were skilled potters and ironworkers. Their terra-cotta (clay) sculptures are known for their high artistic and technological standards.

People continued to settle in the land that is now Nigeria. Those in the northern savanna carried on trade between North Africa and Nigeria's central forestlands. Meanwhile, groups in the south thrived on farming and coastal trading.

Southern Kingdoms

Many ethnic groups in today's Nigeria trace their origins to early kingdoms and states. The earliest kingdom was the Igbo kingdom of Nri, in the southeast. Nri culture flourished long before 1043, when the first Nri ruler,

Opposite: **This terra-cotta head from the Nok culture was made between 1,000 and 1,800 years ago.**

This sculpture of a queen is from the kingdom of Benin, which flourished in Nigeria in the 1400s and 1500s.

Ìfikuánim, gained power. His successors ruled large parts of today's Igbo territory until the early 1900s.

By the 1100s, people of the southwestern forests were united as the Yoruba Kingdom under their first king, Oduduwa. Well governed and highly organized, the kingdom was powerful. Its farmers grew abundant crops, and its craftspeople produced exquisite artworks in bronze, brass, copper, wood, ceramic, and ivory. Ife was the Yoruba cultural and spiritual center, and the *Ooni* (king) of Ife is still regarded as a spiritual leader.

Southwest of Ife lived the Edo people. Also known as the Bini, the Edo people are related to the Yoruba. They created the kingdom of Benin, which reached its height in the 1400s and 1500s. With its capital at today's Benin City, the Benin Kingdom flourished as a center of trade and craftsmanship. Artisans produced impressive bronze sculptures known today as the Benin bronzes.

In the 1400s, the rulers of the Yoruba Kingdom shifted north from Ife to Oyo. The city grew as a military,

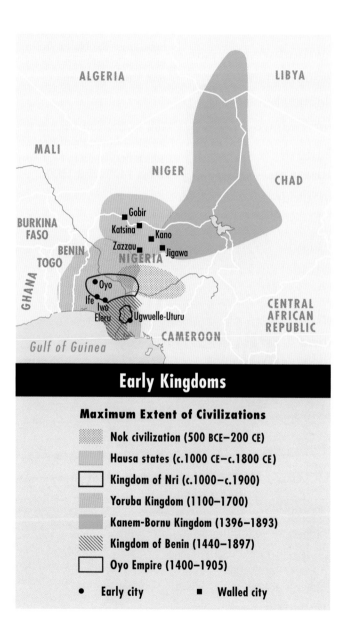

Early Kingdoms

Maximum Extent of Civilizations

- Nok civilization (500 BCE–200 CE)
- Hausa states (c.1000 CE–c.1800 CE)
- Kingdom of Nri (c.1000–c.1900)
- Yoruba Kingdom (1100–1700)
- Kanem-Bornu Kingdom (1396–1893)
- Kingdom of Benin (1440–1897)
- Oyo Empire (1400–1905)
- ● Early city ■ Walled city

agricultural, and trade center. The Oyo Empire emerged, and it eventually gained control of many nearby kingdoms.

Igbo ceramics often featured geometric designs.

This ornament shaped like a
hornbill bird was used long
ago by Hausa dancers.

Kanem, a kingdom northeast of Lake Chad, began to rise around 700 CE. Its people converted from their traditional religions to Islam in the 1000s. The kingdom became wealthy from its trade in ostrich feathers, enslaved people, and ivory. Kanem gradually expanded westward until, by the late 1300s, it was centered in Bornu (today's Borno). The Kanem-Bornu Kingdom carried on trade both within Africa and with European and Asian countries.

Meanwhile, Hausa farmers were settling in communities west of Bornu. By about 1100, they had formed several Hausa states with walled cities, including Kano, Katsina, Jigawa, Gobir, and Zazzau (now Zaria). Each state had a specialty. For example, Kano focused on leatherwork and weaving, while Zazzau specialized in capturing people from the southern forestlands to trade as slaves in markets to the north. By the 1400s, many Hausa rulers had accepted Islam. Gradually, Fulani people began to move into Hausa territory. The Fulani were nomadic herders, though some settled among the Hausa, converted to the religion of Islam, and became prominent citizens.

Many other kingdoms and states flourished before the 1500s. In central Nigeria, the Nupe formed the Nupe Kingdom, and the Jukun people created the states of Kwararafa, Kona, Pinduga, and Wukari. In the south were the Efik people's Calabar Kingdom and the Itsekiri state of Warri. Soon the arrival of Europeans would have an impact on them all.

The Slave Trade

The Portuguese were the first Europeans to reach Nigeria. Portuguese trading ships arrived in 1472. They landed near Benin City, where they established a slave trade with the Benin Kingdom. Dutch, French, British, and other traders soon joined in the trade, too. The southwestern coast became known as the Slave Coast, and chiefs and kings accumulated great wealth by capturing people and selling them to the Europeans. The Benin and the Oyo kingdoms were major suppliers, taking slaves most heavily from the Yoruba and the Igbo groups. Slave traders captured people, chained them together with iron neck rings, and forced them to march hundreds of miles to the coastal slave forts. Then, the people were crammed into slave ships for the long trip across the Atlantic Ocean. By the 1700s, the British had edged out their competitors and gained control of the entire slave trade.

While the slave trade flourished in the south, a revolution was brewing in the north. Over time, the Hausa governments had become lax and corrupt. This paved the way for a Fulani religious reformer named Usman dan Fodio. In 1804, he launched a jihad, or holy war, and took over the Hausa states. He was able to unite them

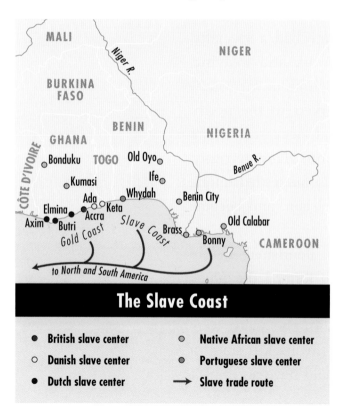

The Slave Coast

- ● British slave center
- ○ Danish slave center
- ● Dutch slave center
- ○ Native African slave center
- ○ Portuguese slave center
- → Slave trade route

Usman dan Fodio: Creating an Empire

Born in the Hausa state of Gobir, Usman dan Fodio (1754–1817) belonged to the class of educated, city-dwelling Fulani. He spent his early years studying Islam under distinguished Muslim scholars. Around age 20, Usman began his own career as a religious teacher, emphasizing piety and strict moral principles. In time, many looked to him for religious and political leadership. In 1804, Usman inspired an uprising among the Fulani and disgruntled Hausa peasants against their oppressive rulers. Usman waged a jihad (holy war) throughout northern Nigeria until 1808, creating a united Fulani empire known as the Sokoto Caliphate. Usman placed community governments in the hands of devout religious leaders, a system still in effect today.

under one rule for the first time. The new empire was called the Sokoto Caliphate.

In 1807, Great Britain outlawed the slave trade. Cruising the coast, the British navy overtook slave ships and set the captured people free in Sierra Leone. British merchants then began trading in Nigeria's farm products.

The British Colony

By the late 1800s, several other European countries were trying to get a foothold in Africa. They met at the 1884–1885 Berlin Conference in Germany and divided up Africa among themselves. Great Britain claimed what is now Nigeria.

In the 1850s, British merchants had set up a trading post at Lokoja, where the Niger and the Benue rivers meet. Britain's Royal Niger Company carried on trade there and served as a government in the region. After making treaties with chiefs to the north and south, the company eventually transferred its territories to the British government.

British officials preside over a court in Nigeria in the 1870s.

At the same time, missionaries from many countries were preaching Christianity among the Yoruba, the Igbo, and other southern groups. The Roman Catholic and Anglican faiths made the strongest inroads. Thus, Nigeria moved forward with a heavily Christian south and a largely Muslim north.

In the early 1900s, the British assumed formal political rule over Nigeria by establishing protectorates—territories that one nation protects against military or diplomatic interference by other nations. The British established the Protectorate of Northern Nigeria in 1900 and the Colony and Protectorate of

Southern Nigeria in 1906. The two were joined in 1914 as the Colony and Protectorate of Nigeria, with its central government in Lagos.

In the 1920s, some Nigerians began to clamor for control of their own government. Two strong Nigerian voices in the growing nationalist movement were Herbert Macaulay and Nnamdi Azikiwe. Macaulay formed the Nigerian National Democratic Party (NNDP) in 1923, and Igbo leader Azikiwe founded the *West African Pilot* newspaper in 1937. The paper was a strong force in building a nationalist spirit. Azikiwe later served in many important government posts and became president of Nigeria.

Independence, Military Rule, and Civil War

As demands for independence grew, Great Britain helped Nigeria draw up a constitution in preparation for self-government. On October 1, 1960, Nigeria officially declared its independence. Each region had its own governor and assembly. At first, the country was divided along ethnic lines

Herbert Macaulay: Father of Nigerian Nationalism

Born in Lagos, Herbert Macaulay (1864–1946) was the grandson of Samuel Crowther, Nigeria's first Anglican bishop. After training in England as a civil engineer, Macaulay worked for the British in Nigeria, but he eventually quit because he strongly opposed British rule. In 1919, Macaulay appealed to the British government on behalf of Yoruba chiefs whose land the British had taken, winning compensation for the chiefs.

Macaulay's popularity grew after this victory, and in 1923 he formed the Nigerian National Democratic Party (NNDP), the first Nigerian political party. He continued to criticize the government in his newspaper, the *Lagos Daily News*. Thanks to Macaulay's inspiration, Nigerians' demand for independence grew stronger over the years. Macaulay is known as the father of Nigerian nationalism.

into three regions—north, southwest, and southeast—for the Hausa, the Yoruba, and the Igbo peoples. Soon, the divisions were changed to four regions. Eventually, there would be 12 states and then, finally, 36 states.

The new nation was wracked with ethnic, regional, and religious tensions. Differences in economic development between north and south only made things worse. Northern Muslims controlled the government, while most of Nigeria's economic resources lay in the south. In 1965, Prime Minister Abubakar Tafawa Balewa retained power in elections that many people considered unfair. The following year, a military group, mainly Igbo officers from the southeast, assassinated Balewa and seized power in a coup, a sudden overthrow of the

Nigerian troops patrol during the Nigerian Civil War. The brutal conflict lasted two and a half years.

government. Later that year, northern Hausa army officers staged a counter-coup, overthrowing the Igbo leaders. During this second coup, thousands of Christian Igbos living in northern regions were killed.

Political and ethnic tensions continued to escalate, and in 1967, the Igbo provinces seceded, declaring themselves the Republic of Biafra. This move exploded into the Nigerian Civil War, also known as the Biafran War (1967–1970). The Biafrans lost, and the bloody conflict left at least one million people dead.

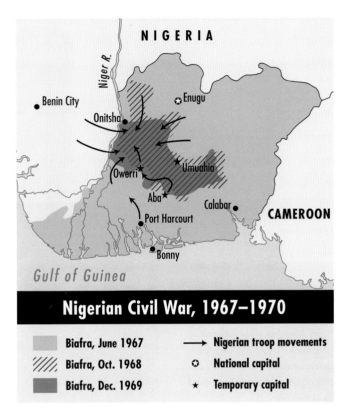

Nigerian Civil War, 1967–1970

Biafra, June 1967	→ Nigerian troop movements
Biafra, Oct. 1968	✪ National capital
Biafra, Dec. 1969	★ Temporary capital

During the next three decades, civilian governments ruled Nigeria for only brief periods. Mostly, Nigeria endured a long string of military dictatorships, coups, and assassinations.

Oil: Boom, Bust, and Exploitation

Oil had been discovered in the Niger Delta in 1908, and commercial oil production got underway in the late 1950s. When world oil prices rose in 1973–1974, Nigeria quickly emerged as one of the top oil producers in the world. Oil became the basis of Nigeria's economy while other industries were neglected. Corruption became rampant as government officials siphoned off the oil profits to enrich themselves.

During his rule, General Sani Abacha stole billions of dollars from the Nigerian government, while much of the nation's population lived in poverty.

Civilians ruled Nigeria briefly, from 1979 to 1983, but then a new military government took over. When world oil prices plummeted in 1982, Nigeria's economy collapsed as well. The country suffered a drastic loss of income, and millions of people were out of work.

General Sani Abacha's regime (1993–1998) was marked by corruption, human rights abuses, and executions of opponents. Billions of dollars of public funds went into his personal accounts. These abuses decreased under Abacha's successor, General Abdulsalami Abubakar. He instituted many reforms, released political prisoners, and set the stage for free democratic elections.

Meanwhile, foreign oil companies were drilling away in the Niger Delta, wreaking havoc on the local people. Families were removed from their land to make way for oil exploration, while oil spills and natural-gas fires ravaged the environment. Their homelands ruined and their soil and water polluted, thousands of people could no longer survive by fishing or farming.

Oil companies drilling in the Niger Delta forced many Nigerians from their homes. Many of them fled into neighboring Benin.

Olusegun Obasanjo worked to end corruption in the Nigerian government during his time as president.

Civilian Government, Oil Wars, and Tough Challenges

In 1999, Nigerians elected Olusegun Obasanjo, a former general, as their first civilian president in 16 years. Obasanjo took over a country in shambles. The government did not work efficiently, roads were in disrepair, and the military still expected to wield power. Obasanjo began investigating human rights violations and allowed more freedom of the press. He released prisoners who had been held without charges and began trying to recover stolen government money.

By 2006, peoples of the Niger Delta had formed several armed militant groups to oppose the oil companies. Most prominent was the Movement for the Emancipation of the Niger Delta (MEND), led by the Ijaw. Its members have destroyed oil refineries and pipelines and attacked Nigerian security forces. They want a fair share of the oil wealth derived from their lands and a halt to the environmental damage caused by oil companies.

When President Umaru Yar'Adua was elected in 2007, it was the first time Nigeria's government had passed from one civilian leader to another. The new president faced many challenges. Muslims and Christians were clashing in the north, non-oil industries were in shambles, and most Nigerians lived in poverty. As militant groups continued their oil wars in the delta, Yar'Adua confessed that the conflict gave him nightmares. Nevertheless, Yar'Adua made a commitment to economic development and peace. Both Nigerians and observers around the world hoped that he would be able to tackle these issues for the sake of Nigeria's future.

President Umaru Yar'Adua worked as a chemistry teacher before entering business and then politics.

Governing the Republic

NIGERIA'S OFFICIAL NAME IS THE FEDERAL REPUBLIC of Nigeria. It is a federal republic, which means that it is a federation, or union, of states in which the government is directed by the people, rather than by a monarch. Nigeria's present constitution went into effect in 1999. It calls for the government to be organized into three branches—executive, legislative, and judicial.

Opposite: **A large dome sits atop the National Assembly Building in Abuja.**

The Executive Branch

Nigeria's president serves as the head of government, the chief of state, and the commander-in-chief of the armed forces. The president is elected to a five-year term and may serve for two terms. Candidates from several different parties usually compete for president. To win the presidency, a candidate must

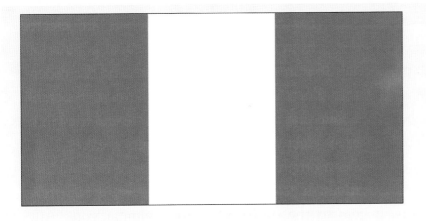

The National Flag

Nigeria's national flag features three vertical stripes of equal width, colored green, white, and green. The white stripe stands for peace and unity. It is also a symbol of the Niger River, which cuts through the countryside. The green stripes represent Nigeria's agriculture. The flag was adopted when Nigeria became independent in 1960.

The National Anthem

John A. Ilechukwu, Eme Etim Akpan, B. A. Ogunnaike, Sotu Omoigui, and P. O. Aderibighe wrote the words to Nigeria's national anthem, "Arise, O Compatriots." Benedict Elide Odiase wrote the music. The song was adopted as the republic's anthem in 1978.

Arise, O compatriots,
Nigeria's call obey
To serve our Fatherland
With love and strength and faith.
The labor of our heroes past
Shall never be in vain,
To serve with heart and might
One nation bound in freedom, peace and unity.

O God of creation,
Direct our noble cause;
Guide our Leaders right:
Help our Youth the truth to know,
In love and honesty to grow,
And living just and true,
Great lofty heights attain,
To build a nation where peace and justice reign.

receive at least one-fourth of the votes in at least two-thirds of Nigeria's 36 states.

Once in office, the president chooses a vice president and a cabinet of government ministers. Cabinet members oversee ministries dealing with agriculture, defense, education, and other areas. All these appointments must be approved by the Senate. Another executive body is the Council of State. It advises the president on the exercise of presidential policy in such matters as national elections.

The Legislative Branch

Lawmaking power rests in the hands of the legislature, which is called the National Assembly. It consists of a 360-member House of Representatives and a 109-member Senate. House members are elected from districts of roughly equal population. Each of Nigeria's 36 states elects three senators, and the Federal Capital Territory elects one senator. All National Assembly members serve four-year terms. Both the Senate and the House of Representatives elect a speaker and a deputy speaker.

A new law can originate in either the Senate or the House of Representatives. If it passes in one house by a two-thirds majority, it goes to the other house for a similar vote. After passing in both houses, the bill goes to the president. Upon the

president's approval, it becomes a law. If the president doesn't approve it, the bill returns to the National Assembly, where both houses cast their votes again. If two-thirds of the members vote yes again, the bill becomes a law.

Legal Systems and the Judicial Branch

Several legal systems are at work in Nigeria. One combines elements of British law with the body of law that has developed from the rulings of judges since Nigeria became independent. Nigeria also respects customary law, or laws derived from the traditional practices of various ethnic groups. Shari'a law, the Muslim legal system, is applied mostly in the north. In 2000, 12 northern states adopted shari'a as part of their legal systems, but it applies only to Muslim residents.

NATIONAL GOVERNMENT OF NIGERIA

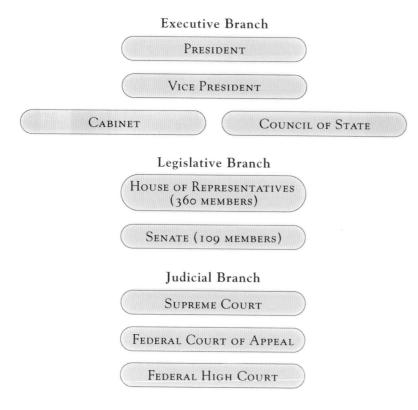

Executive Branch

PRESIDENT

VICE PRESIDENT

CABINET   COUNCIL OF STATE

Legislative Branch

HOUSE OF REPRESENTATIVES
(360 MEMBERS)

SENATE (109 MEMBERS)

Judicial Branch

SUPREME COURT

FEDERAL COURT OF APPEAL

FEDERAL HIGH COURT

The judicial branch of Nigeria's government is made up of its national and state court systems. The highest court is the Supreme Court, with a chief justice and up to 21 associate justices. All are appointed by the president on the recommendation of the National Judicial Council and approved by the Senate. The Supreme Court hears disputes between state and federal governments and between two states. It also reviews decisions made in the Federal Court of Appeal.

The Federal Court of Appeal has a president and at least 35 justices. Three of them must be experts in shari'a law, and 3 must specialize in customary law. This court hears appeals from state courts and other lower courts. A third national-level court is the Federal High Court, with a chief judge and several other judges. They deal with civil (noncriminal) cases and matters such as taxation, banking, and citizenship.

Each state has a high court and, if necessary, a shari'a court of appeal and a customary court of appeal.

Local Government

Nigeria is divided into 36 states plus the Federal Capital Territory, the district surrounding the national capital of Abuja. States are further divided into a total of 774 local government areas (LGAs), and each LGA is divided into 10 to 15 wards. Voters in each state elect a governor and a House of Assembly. State assemblies are composed of 24 to 40 members.

In each LGA, voters elect members to serve on a local government council. The council members have a wide range of duties. They give the state government recommendations for economic improvements in their area. They also collect taxes; issue licenses to vehicles as diverse as trucks, bicycles, wheelbarrows, and canoes; maintain roads and parks; and regulate shops, restaurants, and even pets. In addition, local councils work with the state on issues such as education, health services, agriculture, and natural resources.

President Yar'Adua

Born into a leading Fulani family, Umaru Musa Yar'Adua (1951–) was elected Nigeria's 13th head of state in 2007. Before that, he served as governor of Katsina State (1999–2007). As president, Yar'Adua took a firm stand against government corruption. He was the first Nigerian president to reveal his financial situation, and he overturned many of the corrupt measures of his predecessor, Olusegun Obasanjo. Yar'Adua also made a commitment to economic development, financial stability, and peace among religious and ethnic groups.

Abuja: Did You Know This?

Abuja replaced Lagos as Nigeria's capital city in 1991. It was chosen because of its central location in the country; its cool, dry climate; and its open surroundings for future development. Located within the Federal Capital Territory, Abuja is designed in several sections, or districts.

The Central District extends south of Aso Rock, a large rock formation on the edge of town. This district is home to the main government and international business operations and various cultural institutes. The district's Three Arms Zone houses the offices of the three branches of national government.

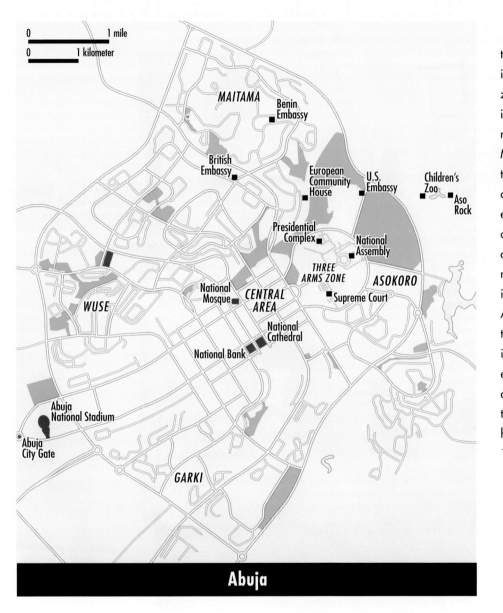

Garki District, to the southwest, is an important business zone. Wuse District, in the northwest, is a major market area. Maitama District, in the north, is the site of many European embassies. The homes of the president and other high government officials are in the upper-class Asokoro District, in the southeast. The city is in the process of expanding into many other districts beyond these. In 2008, Abuja had a population of 1,129,345.

A Struggling Economy

NIGERIA IS RICH IN NATURAL RESOURCES. IT IS THE largest oil producer in Africa, with the world's 10th-largest oil reserves and 7th-largest natural gas reserves. The country also has an abundance of fertile land.

Despite its wealth, however, Nigeria is a poor country. More than half the people live in poverty, surviving on the equivalent of less than one U.S. dollar a day. Today, Nigeria's government is taking measures to diversify the economy and improve Nigerians' quality of life.

Opposite: **Nigeria's oil industry is based in the Niger Delta. The country's oil wells are among the most productive in the world.**

Many Nigerians live in slums in Lagos.

Mining

Oil, or petroleum, is Nigeria's most valuable product by far. In 2006, it accounted for about 98 percent of the country's export earnings, with exports of more than 2 million barrels of oil a day. (One barrel is equal to 42 U.S. gallons, or 159 liters.)

The Nigerian National Petroleum Corporation (NNPC) regulates the country's oil industry. NNPC partners with several foreign oil companies, including Shell, Chevron, and ExxonMobil. About two-thirds of Nigeria's oil production takes place on land, although offshore oil drilling in the Gulf of Guinea is increasing. Most onshore oil fields and refineries are located in the Niger Delta.

An offshore oil drilling platform sits above the water in the Gulf of Guinea, near the Nigerian coast.

Gas Flaring: Energy Going Up in Smoke

Travel through the Niger Delta, and you come upon enormous flames reaching to the sky. Some flames pour out of holes in the ground, while others shoot from smokestacks. These flames are gas flares—fires set to burn off the natural gas in oil fields. The fires are so huge that they can be seen on satellite images taken from space.

Gas flaring is a tremendous waste of a valuable energy resource. This gas could be used as a source of energy for homes in the region, most of which have no electricity. The smoke from the oil fields also pours tons of pollution into the atmosphere. Many villagers in the delta complain of breathing problems and withering crops because of the flares. Nigeria is pressuring oil companies to stop gas flaring, but the practice continues.

Most of Nigeria's vast natural gas reserves are also located in the Niger Delta. Natural gas usually occurs in the same places as oil. But many oil companies are not set up to process natural gas. They see the gas as an unwanted by-product, and they set it on fire to remove it from the oil. Some of Nigeria's natural gas is processed into liquefied natural gas (LNG). LNG is natural gas that has been cooled to an extremely low temperature to condense it to liquid form. It is mostly used to fuel buses, trucks, and other heavy-duty vehicles. Plans are underway to deliver natural gas by pipeline to other West African countries.

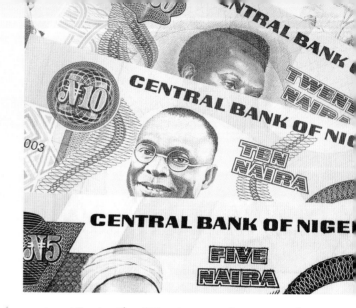

Money Facts

Nigeria's basic unit of currency is the naira, which is divided into 100 kobo. Banknotes come in denominations of 5, 10, 20, 50, 100, 200, 500, and 1000 naira, and coins have values of 50 kobo, 1 naira, and 2 naira. In April 2009, 1 naira was equal to US$0.007, and US$1.00 was equal to 147.2 naira.

Most Nigerian banknotes feature a historic political leader on the front and an economic or cultural activity or geographical landmark on the back. For example, the front of the 5-naira note pictures Abubakar Tafawa Balewa, independent Nigeria's first prime minister. On the back are Nkpokiti drummers and dancers of south-eastern Nigeria. The 500-naira note shows Nnamdi Azikiwe, Nigeria's first president, on the front and an offshore oil platform on the back.

Nigeria is rich in many other minerals, but few of them are mined because of the emphasis on oil. The country has significant coal reserves, and a coal-mining industry is gradually developing. Tin, columbite, iron ore, gypsum, limestone, gold, and gemstones are mined on a small scale.

Workers use a drill to uncover tin buried underground. Nigeria produces about 1,500 metric tons of tin per year.

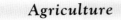

Agriculture

Agriculture was once a thriving industry in Nigeria. The country's farmers produced enough not only to feed Nigerians but also to export foods to other countries. After the oil boom of the 1970s, however, thousands of rural people left their farms and moved to the cities for jobs in the oil, manufacturing, and construction industries. Agriculture was neglected and poorly managed for years. As a result, Nigeria now has to import much of its own food.

About two-thirds of the nation's labor force works in agriculture. Most farms are small, and most farmers work their fields with old-fashioned tools such as hoes and machetes.

With Nigeria's diverse climate, farmers are able to raise a wide variety of crops. One widespread crop is cassava, or manioc. This starchy root is a staple food for Nigerians, providing the basis of their diet. Nigeria is the world's largest producer of cassava.

In the south, where rainfall is heaviest, the most important food crops are root plants such as yams, cassava, taro, and sweet potatoes. Southern farmers also grow palm, cacao, rubber, and cashew trees. Cacao trees produce cocoa beans, which

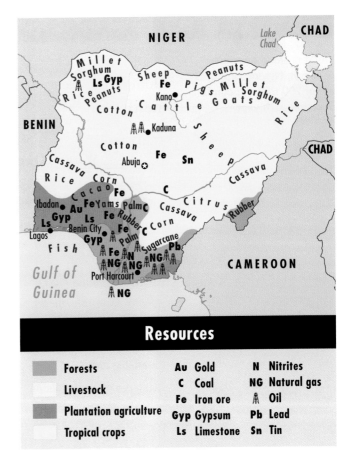

Resources

Forests	**Au** Gold	**N** Nitrites
Livestock	**C** Coal	**NG** Natural gas
	Fe Iron ore	Oil
Plantation agriculture	**Gyp** Gypsum	**Pb** Lead
Tropical crops	**Ls** Limestone	**Sn** Tin

Workers stand near piles of cotton. Nigeria produces about 200 million pounds of cotton each year.

are used to make chocolate. Cocoa and rubber are leading agricultural exports.

In the drier north, the main food crops are legumes such as cowpeas and grains such as Guinea corn (a type of sorghum), millet, and corn. Guinea corn is a drought-resistant grain that thrives in dry climates. People make it into porridge, biscuits, and dumplings. Peanuts and cotton are important crops in the north, too.

What Nigeria Grows, Makes, and Mines

Agriculture (2006)

Cassava	45,721,000 metric tons
Yams	36,720,000 metric tons
Sorghum	9,866,000 metric tons

Manufacturing (2003)

Gasoline, diesel, and other petroleum fuels	70,000,000 barrels
Cement	2,100,000 metric tons
Wheat flour	1,598,000 metric tons

Mining (2006)

Crude petroleum	813,950,000 barrels
Natural gas	57,754,000,000 cubic meters
Gypsum	160,000 metric tons

One of the most valuable crops in Nigeria's middle belt is sesame. Its oily seed is used in baking, made into cooking oil, and processed as a base for soaps and medicines. Farmers in the middle belt grow about half the country's soybeans, too. They also raise yams, sorghum, millet, cassava, cowpeas, and corn.

Other Nigerian crops include sugarcane, rice, tomatoes, oranges, guavas, mangoes, and plantains, a type of banana. Some Nigerians also raise cattle, chickens, sheep, goats, and pigs. The Fulani herders of northern Nigeria produce most of the nation's beef cattle.

A Fulani herder tends cattle in central Nigeria. There are about 16 million cattle in Nigeria.

Manufacturing

Much of Nigeria's manufacturing activity is related to the petroleum industry. Oil refineries take crude oil and process it into a variety of products, including gasoline, kerosene, and diesel fuel. Like agriculture, nonpetroleum manufacturing fell into decline with the oil boom of the 1970s.

Nigeria's food plants process meat, grains, fruits, vegetables, and other farm products. They turn out foods such as milk, palm oil, sugar, flour, animal feed, bakery goods, chocolate, and beverages. Steel mills process iron ore into steel, and wood-processing plants produce plywood, paper, and cardboard. The country also has several motor vehicle assembly plants. Other factories make cement, tires, textiles and clothing, metal products, leather goods such as shoes and luggage, and chemical products such as medicines, fertilizer, and paint.

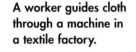

A worker guides cloth through a machine in a textile factory.

Many Nigerians carry on small industries from their homes. They make soap, table salt, and iron tools such as hoes and door hinges. Many craftspeople in rural areas make pottery, woodcarvings, or wooden furniture. Others weave raffia, a fiber of the raffia palm, into mats, baskets, handbags, and hats.

Many Nigerians often travel on foot. These women balance enormous containers on their heads on their way to a market.

Services

People who work in the service industry provide helpful services instead of producing goods. About one out of five Nigerian workers is a service worker. Banking is an important branch of the service industry. Hundreds of community banks are scattered throughout the country, and large city banks provide loans for development projects. Other service workers include schoolteachers, health care workers, shopkeepers, mechanics, restaurant and hotel workers, and government employees, including postal workers and military personnel.

Transportation

Paved roads connect the major cities in Nigeria. Cars, motorcycles, and motor scooters are common on highways and city streets. Motorcycles, known as *okadas*, function as taxis, taking passengers from one part of town to another or one village to another. People also jam into buses to travel between towns. Alongside the roads, people travel to market on foot, carrying loads of firewood and bundles of crops.

Only about 15 percent of Nigeria's roads are paved. Beyond the major road network, people travel on unpaved dirt trails. Even the paved roads can offer a rough ride. In some places, the potholes are bigger than cars. Climate conditions affect

Philip Emeagwali: Superscientist

Born in Akure, Philip Emeagwali (1954–) is a member of the Igbo ethnic group. During the Nigerian Civil War, his family lived in refugee camps, and at age 14 he was drafted to serve in the Biafran army.

Emeagwali continued studying on his own, completed his high school equivalency, and received a scholarship to Oregon State University, where he earned a bachelor's degree in mathematics. He later earned two master's degrees, one in mathematics and one in in environmental engineering. In 1989, he won supercomputing's Gordon Bell Prize for designing a computer network that performed calculations to locate oil reserves. His method was faster, more accurate, and more cost-effective than any previous systems. In 2004, the New African magazine named Emeagwali one of the greatest Africans of all time.

transportation, too. During the rainy season, roads in the south become too muddy or flooded to be reliable.

Nigeria has about 70 airports. The major international airports are in Lagos, Kano, and Abuja. Kaduna and Port Harcourt also have international air service.

Nigeria's major shipping ports are in the Niger Delta. The largest are at Lagos, Port Harcourt, Calabar, Warri, and Sapele. Major railroad lines run from Lagos and Port Harcourt to the northern part of the country.

Communications

To contact one another, far more Nigerians use cell phones than landline phones. In 2007, more than 40 million Nigerians used cell phones. Although there are few computers in the country, Internet use is heavy. Because few people can afford to buy computers, they rely on Internet cafés.

Most Nigerians get their news from radio and television. Nigeria has more than 100 radio stations, most of which are run by the government. They broadcast programs in several local languages. The national government owns two TV stations, many states have their own stations, and some private TV companies broadcast programs by satellite.

More than 20 daily newspapers are published in Nigeria. Those with the most readers are the *Daily Times*, the *National Concord*, the *Daily Champion*, the *Nigerian Observer*, and *The Punch*. Only one daily paper, the *New Nigerian*, is government owned. This means that newspapers are a better outlet than radio or TV for commentators who want to discuss government policies freely. A lively dialogue on public issues may help Nigeria sustain its newfound democracy.

Many Nigerians get their news from newspapers. Nigeria has the second-largest newspaper circulation of any country in Africa, trailing only Egypt.

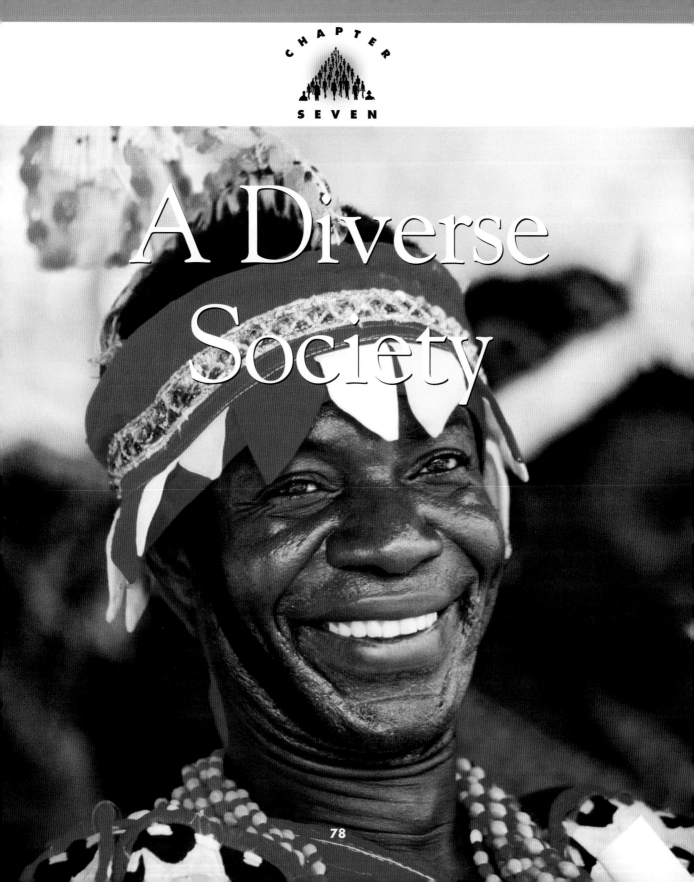

A Diverse
Society

WITH MORE THAN 140 MILLION PEOPLE, NIGERIA IS the eighth most populous country in the world. It is also the most populous country in Africa: about one out of every six Africans is a Nigerian. It would be impossible to describe a typical Nigerian because of the country's rich ethnic diversity. Within the country's borders is an extraordinary range of peoples, languages, beliefs, customs, and value systems. Each group forges relationships with others to coexist within a unified nation.

Opposite: **A man dressed in traditional clothing attends a Nigerian festival.**

Traffic sometimes comes to a standstill in Lagos and other large Nigerian cities.

Population of Largest Cities (2008 est.)

Lagos	9,494,045
Ibadan	4,826,891
Kano	2,330,412
Benin City	2,238,589
Kaduna	1,926,356

Nigeria's Ethnic Groups

Hausa-Fulani	29%
Yoruba	21%
Igbo (Ibo)	18%
Ijaw	10%
Kanuri	4%
Ibibio	3.5%
Tiv	2.5%
Other	12%

Nigeria is home to more than 300 ethnic groups. The most populous groups are the Hausa and Fulani, the Yoruba, and the Igbo (also spelled Ibo). Each group has its unique history, culture, and traditions.

The Hausa and Fulani

Hausa and Fulani people make up about 29 percent of the population. They are concentrated in northern Nigeria. The two are grouped together because their histories and cultures have been interwoven for so long. After the Fulani overtook the Hausa kingdoms in the early 1800s, Hausa-speaking Fulani emirs ruled states called emirates. Emirs are still the traditional rulers in many northern cities and states.

The Hausa and the Fulani are both largely Muslim. They share many cultural traditions, and intermarriage between them is common. They have blended together so well that they are often called the Hausa-Fulani. Hausa-Fulani leaders have controlled national politics for much of Nigeria's history since independence.

Hausa people are the largest ethnic group in West Africa, and about nine-tenths of them live in northern Nigeria, often called Hausaland.

Ethnic Groups

Hausa-Fulani	Ijaw	Yoruba
Ibibio	Kanuri	Other/mixed
Igbo (Ibo)	Tiv	Edo Ethnic group

A Fulani boy keeps watch over his family's cattle.

Throughout history, the Hausa have worked as traders, and for centuries Kano was their center of trade and culture. Most Hausa people live in small villages, where they farm and raise livestock.

The Fulani were traditionally nomadic cattle herders. Most of Nigeria's Fulani have settled in cities and towns, and many Fulani families belong to the ruling class. However, some Fulani still hold onto their herding lifestyle. The Fulani maintain their identity through a code of ethics called *pulaaku*. It involves the virtues of *munyal* (patience, courage, and mental discipline), *semteende* (modesty, self-control, and respect for others), and *hakkille* (wisdom and common sense).

Yoruba people gather for a festival. The Yoruba are the largest ethnic group in southwestern Nigeria.

The Yoruba

Yoruba people make up about 21 percent of the population. Their traditional homeland is southwestern Nigeria, which is often called Yorubaland. Major Yoruba cities include Lagos, Ibadan, Ife, and Abeokuta. Many Yoruba towns and ethnic subgroups have an honorary ruler called the *oba* (king). Although obas are not part of the government structure, they command great authority and respect among their people.

The ancient city of Ife is the Yorubas' traditional capital. According to Yoruba religion, Ife was founded by Oduduwa, the creator of all humanity. A religious leader called the Ooni of Ife is considered a descendant of Oduduwa. He is the traditional ruler of the Yoruba people and a powerful spiritual figure. Today, most Yoruba people are either Christian or Muslim, but traditional beliefs remain a part of Yoruba culture.

Twins (*ibeji*) have a special place in Yoruba culture. The Yoruba have the world's highest birthrate of twins, with 45 sets of twins per 1,000 births. (About 90 percent of them are fraternal twins, rather than identical twins.) In the United States, the average is 12 sets of twins per 1,000 births. For the Yoruba, twins have the spiritual power to bring good fortune to the family. Twins are also believed to share one soul. Unfortunately, the infant death rate in Nigeria is high, so one of the twins may die. In that case, a wooden carving called *ere ibiji* is made of the deceased twin to keep the soul in balance. The parents continue to care for this image as if the twin were still alive.

The Igbo

About 18 percent of Nigerians are Igbo. ("Igbo" is pronounced *EE-boh*, so it's sometimes spelled *Ibo*.) They are concentrated in the southeast, in the dense forestlands around and east of

The Last Becomes First

The Yoruba people have special names that are used for twins. The firstborn twin is traditionally called Taiwo, meaning "The First to Taste the World." The name for the second-born twin is Kehinde, which means "Arriving After Another Person." Although born second, Kehinde is considered the senior twin.

According to Yoruba tradition, Kehinde is older than Taiwo before birth. But Kehinde sends Taiwo out first to check and see if the world is a good place. In Yoruba culture, sending someone on such an errand is a privilege of elders. Taiwo's first cry tells Kehinde what the world is like.

the Niger River. Igbo territory is known as Igboland. Major Igbo cities include Owerri, Enugu, Aba, Umuahia, Port Harcourt, and Asaba. Although the Igbo are predominantly Christian, their traditional culture and religion remain strong, especially in rural villages.

Because their land is so fertile, most Igbo live as farmers. The yam is their staple crop, and they celebrate the New Yam Festival at harvesttime. Women and men are equally involved in community functions such as farming, trading, and priestly activities. Exceptions are that warriors are men and healers are women.

Some Igbo people dance at a New Year's celebration.

Igbo people belong to age-grade groups based on three-year periods, such as 18- to 21-year-olds. Each age-grade is responsible for certain tasks. In Abiriba, for example, various age-grades have built schools, hospitals, and stadiums. Special ceremonies mark the handing over of one age-grade's responsibilities to another.

Other Ethnic Groups

Many other ethnic groups make their homes in Nigeria. A large population of Kanuri people live in the northeast, where the Kanem-Bornu Kingdom once flourished. The Kanuri are largely Muslim. They farm the sandy soil, raising millet and peanuts and trading with nearby groups.

North-central Nigeria, the so-called middle belt, is quite diverse, with more than 150 ethnic groups. Most numerous are the Tiv and the Nupe, who live as farmers. The Tiv live alongside the Benue River, cultivating yams and cassava as well as grains, peanuts, and vegetables. Most Nupe people are Muslim, and Bida is their major city.

The Ibibio and an offshoot group, the Efik people, live near the Igbo, especially in Cross River State. Many occupy farming villages in the rain forest, cultivating oil palms, yams, and cassava. The far south, in the Niger Delta region, is home to Ijaw, Edo, Itsekiri, Ekol, and many other groups. The Ijaw live among the swamps and creeks of the delta. They rely on fishing, farming, and trading in yams and palm oil.

The Edo occupy villages west of the Niger River. Most Edo people live as farmers, raising crops and livestock. Men

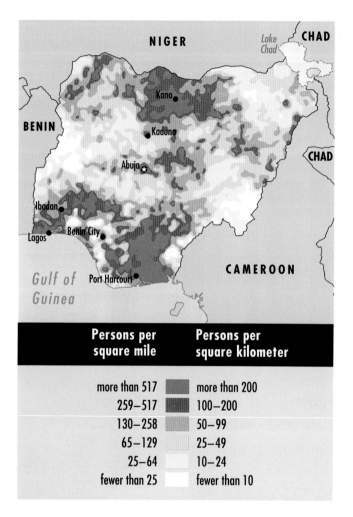

Persons per square mile	Persons per square kilometer
more than 517	more than 200
259–517	100–200
130–258	50–99
65–129	25–49
25–64	10–24
fewer than 25	fewer than 10

and boys are divided into age-grades with tasks such as clearing paths and maintaining buildings. Benin City is the capital of Edo territory, as it was in the days of the Benin Kingdom. Edo artisans are known for their brass, wood, leather, and textile crafts.

Speaking in Many Tongues

In Nigeria, English is the official language used in government and education. But Nigeria is such an ethnically diverse country that Nigerians speak many other languages, and English is a second language for most people. In all, more than 500 languages are spoken in Nigeria. Three of those languages have more than 18 million speakers each: Hausa, Yoruba, and Igbo. Each major language has several regional dialects, or variations.

Hausa is commonly spoken in the northern half of Nigeria, where it is the customary language for trade, education, and government. Hausa is a tonal language, in which words have different meanings depending on the high, low, or falling tone of the vowel sounds. Various consonant sounds are stopped in the throat, rather than breathed through, as they are in

English. The Hausa alphabet, called *boko*, has 29 characters. Hausa has also sometimes been written in *ajami*, a variation of ornate Arabic script.

Yoruba is widespread in southwestern Nigeria. Government notices often appear in Yoruba. This region also has Yoruba-language newspapers, radio programs, and TV shows. Yoruba is taught in primary and secondary schools in the southwest, too. Its alphabet, based on the common Latin alphabet, has 25 characters. Yoruba is also a tonal language, with vowels having high, middle, low, and rising tones. Depending on the vowel tones, for example, the word *ogun* can mean "a fishing basket," "an inheritance," "medicine," "sweat," "war," or "twenty."

An election poster includes phrases in both English and Yoruba.

Igbo is the most common language in the southeast. It is written in the *onwu* alphabet, which has 36 characters. Some of the characters stand for blended sounds, such as the sounds of *ng, ny, gb,* and *kp.* Igbo is also tonal, with high and low vowel sounds.

Fulfulde, the native language of the Fulani people, is widely spoken as well. Anaang, Ebira, Edo, Ibibio, Izon, and Kanuri all have more than 1 million speakers each. These and many other regional languages are taught in local schools and broadcast on radio and TV programs.

Many Nigerians speak two or more languages. Living side by side with diverse peoples for centuries, they learned the value of communicating with their neighbors.

A teacher fills out a form for a new student. In Nigeria, children start school at age six.

Nigerian schoolchildren listen as their teacher instructs them on the English language.

Education

All children ages 6 through 15 are required to attend school, and public schools are free up to that point. Primary school lasts for six years, from ages 6 through 12. Classes are taught in the local language for the first three years and in English after that. Secondary school is broken into two stages of three years each. After junior secondary school, students take an exam for entry into senior secondary school.

Primary and secondary schools require children to wear school uniforms. They also have strict rules about hairstyles, jewelry, and shoes. Families who can afford it send their

A Diverse Society **89**

Many Nigerian children attend Qur'anic schools, which help them learn the teachings of the Muslim faith.

children to private schools or boarding schools. Christian churches or private organizations run these schools. In the north, many Muslim children attend Qur'anic schools, where they get a religious education. Some go to both religious and academic schools, while others attend only Qur'anic schools.

School Attendance: A Nationwide Dilemma

Although school is required, only about 60 percent of Nigerian children attend primary school, according to a 2004 study. There are various reasons why children do not go to school. Some parents need their children to work at home or earn money to support the family. The school may be so far away that it takes too long to walk there. The family may not have the money for school fees and supplies. Parents may feel that the school does not offer good-quality instruction.

City children are more likely to go to school than children in rural areas. In secondary schools, attendance is much lower. Nationwide, only about 35 percent of children attend secondary school. A family's economic condition has a drastic impact on whether children go to school. Only 15 percent of kids from the lowest income level attend secondary school. Nigeria's education department is using these findings to try to improve the state of education in the country.

Nigeria has more than 50 universities and many more teachers' colleges, technical institutes, and vocational schools. Nigeria's first university, the University of Ibadan, was founded in 1948. Prominent universities today include the University of Nigeria in Nsukka, Obafemi Awolowo University in Ife, Ahmadu Bello University in Zaria, and the University of Lagos. A number of universities specialize in agriculture or science and technology.

The African University of Science and Technology opened in Abuja in 2008. It is the first in a network of research-oriented institutes to be built across Africa to train scientists and engineers. Nigerians welcome this opportunity to meet the high-tech challenges of the future.

A student at the Federal Advanced Teachers College in Lagos takes notes during a lecture.

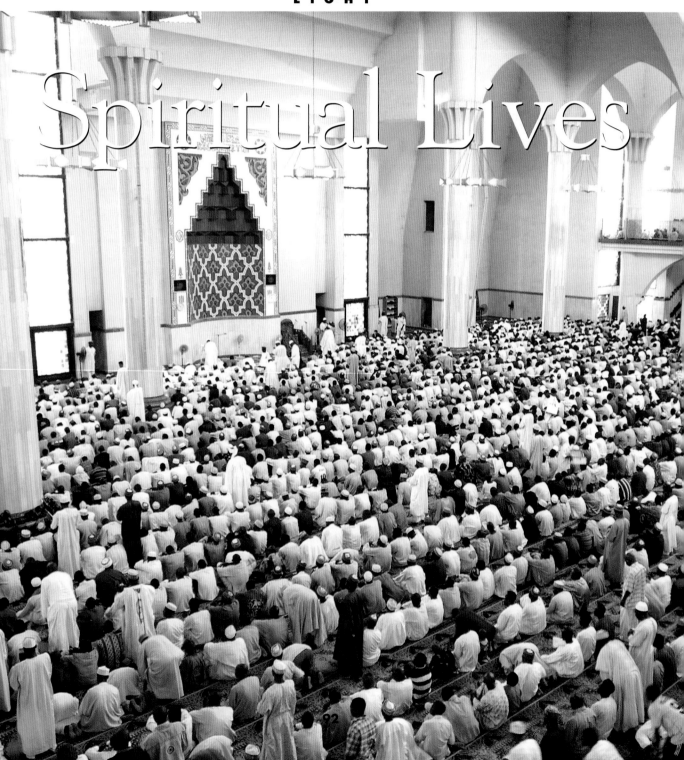

Spiritual Lives

R ELIGION IN NIGERIA IS TIED TO ETHNIC GROUPS AND regional divisions. Northern Nigeria's Hausa and Fulani peoples are largely Muslims, or followers of Islam. Christianity has a strong following among ethnic groups in the south. The two faiths converge along Nigeria's middle belt.

Religious beliefs in the southwest are mixed, with the Yoruba people following Islam, Christianity, or the traditional Yoruba religion. Other ethnic groups follow ancient beliefs as well. These deep-seated cultural influences persist, even among those who have adopted a new faith. Many people who profess faith in Islam or Christianity include elements of traditional beliefs in their practice.

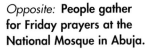

Opposite: **People gather for Friday prayers at the National Mosque in Abuja.**

A man prays at a mosque in northern Nigeria.

Major Religions of Nigeria

Islam	50%
Christianity	40%
Traditional religions	10%

Islam is the most common religion in Nigeria, with Muslims making up about 50 percent of the population. About 40 percent of Nigerians are Christians, and the remaining 10 percent follow various traditional religions.

Islam

Islam arrived in northern Nigeria as early as the 800s CE, as Arab traders helped spread their religion from town to town. They brought their faith from Arabia, where the Prophet Muhammad had founded Islam in the 600s. Both the Hausa states and the Kanem-Bornu Kingdom embraced Islam. Under the Sokoto Caliphate, founded by Usman dan Fodio in the early 1800s, much of northern Nigeria was united as an Islamic domain.

For Muslims, the teachings of God are set forth in the Qur'an, Islam's holy book. Friday is Muslims' holy day,

The Sultan of Sokoto

Muhammadu Sa'adu Abubakar was born in Sokoto in 1956. He is a great-grandson of Usman dan Fodio and son of the popular Siddiq Abu Bakar dan Usuman, who was known for his peace efforts during his 50-year reign (1938–1988). In 2006, Abubakar became the 20th sultan of Sokoto. As such, he is the spiritual leader of Nigeria's Muslims. A career military officer, Abubakar led peacekeeping forces in Chad and Sierra Leone and was Nigeria's military representative to Pakistan before becoming sultan. Since assuming his position, he has made religious harmony between Muslims and Christians one of his highest priorities.

and mosques are their houses of worship. Domed mosques with towers, or minarets, rise in every Muslim city and town in Nigeria. From the minaret, a muezzin calls the faithful to prayer five times a day. Loudspeakers carry the piercing cry of the muezzin throughout the city. Then men stop their tasks, lay out their prayer rugs, and kneel and bow in prayer, facing the holy city of Mecca in Saudi Arabia.

Most of Nigeria's Muslims belong to the Sunni sect of Islam, but a smaller number follow the Shi'i sect. Differences between the two date back to a centuries-old disagreement about Muhammad's successor. Most Shi'i live in Kano and Sokoto states. Sokoto is the center of Islamic activities in Nigeria. It is the home of the sultan of Sokoto, the spiritual leader of Nigerian Muslims. This position is still held by descendants of Usman dan Fodio.

Minarets tower above a mosque in Kano.

Muslim Holidays

The Islamic calendar is a lunar calendar, based on phases of the moon. Thus, Muslim religious holidays do not fall on the same days every year. The two most important feast days are also Nigerian national holidays: 'Id al-Fitr and 'Id al-Kabir. 'Id al-Fitr marks the end of the holy month of Ramadan. During this month, when Muslims believe the Qur'an was revealed

A chief rides a decorated horse during a Durbar festival.

to Muhammad, the faithful fast from dawn until sunset. At the end of the month, people celebrate 'Id al-Fitr by donning their finest clothes, greeting one another and presenting gifts, and joining in prayers of praise.

'Id al-Kabir, the Feast of the Sacrifice, is often called Babbar Sallah in Nigeria. It commemorates the prophet Abraham's willingness to sacrifice his son out of faith in God. 'Id al-Kabir is also the time for the hajj, a pilgrimage to the holy city of Mecca in today's Saudi Arabia. All Muslims are obliged to make this trip at least once in their lifetime if they are able to do so.

These two holidays are celebrated together in a spectacular festival called Durbar. Durbar dates from the time of horseback warriors who paraded before their chiefs. Today's Durbar festivals are shows of horsemanship, with ornately dressed swordsmen parading on their horses before emirs and other dignitaries. Katsina's Durbar is the most magnificent, and others are held in northern cities such as Kano, Bauchi, and Bida.

Christianity

Christianity reached southern Nigeria as early as the 1400s, when Portuguese traders first arrived. By the 1800s, Christian missionaries of many denominations were sailing into Nigerian ports. Besides teaching their faith in remote areas, missionaries also opened schools and health care facilities.

Today, the largest Christian groups in Nigeria are Roman Catholics and Anglicans. Catholicism is strongest among the Igbo in the southeast, whereas Anglicanism is common among the Yoruba of the southwest. The Anglican Church, or Church of England, is known in Nigeria as the Church of Nigeria. Presbyterian missionaries gained many followers among the Ibibio, the Anaang, and other groups in the Niger Delta region. Baptist, Lutheran, Methodist, Brethren, and Assembly of God churches made strong inroads, too.

Samuel Crowther: First African Anglican Bishop

When Samuel Crowther (c. 1809–1891) was born, he was named Ajayi. He was a Yoruba from Osogun, in what is now western Nigeria. When he was about 12, he was kidnapped and sold to Portuguese slave traders. The British overtook the slave ship and released Ajayi in Sierra Leone, where Anglican missionaries taught him English. At around age 16, he converted to Anglicanism and took the name Samuel Crowther. Later, he traveled to England, where he was trained and ordained as an Anglican minister. As a missionary in the Niger River valley, he worked to combat the slave trade, help newly freed people, and wipe out witchcraft practices. An expert in languages, Crowther translated the Bible into Yoruba and compiled dictionaries in the Yoruba, Igbo, and Nupe languages. In 1864, he was ordained the first African bishop of the Anglican Church.

Since the 1980s, Pentecostal and evangelical churches have spread quickly in the south, spilling northward into the middle belt. Both groups emphasize a direct relationship with God, the authority of the Bible, and conversion by being "born again."

The Aladura Church, or Church of the Lord, has been growing fast in Yoruba areas. It is one of several Africanized Christian churches that broke away from standard Christian denominations. These churches blend Christianity and indigenous religions, often with an evangelical element. Some rely on faith healing and prayer, while others focus on visions, dreams, secret rituals, and driving out witches and demons.

A group of women from an Aladura church pray together on a beach. Aladura churches were first established in the 1920s.

Christian Holidays

Christmas is a national holiday in Nigeria. Throughout the country, streets are aglitter with decorations and bright lights. Palm branches, a symbol of peace, adorn homes, churches, and shops. People travel long distances to their home villages to reunite with loved ones and exchange gifts. Among Catholics, midnight mass may be the main religious service, while other Christians attend services on Christmas morning. Then, people enjoy a big feast of meats, yams, boiled rice, and spicy stew, topped off by Christmas cake.

A group of Nigerian Christians celebrate Easter with a special prayer service.

Some families hold Christmas Eve parties that last all through the night, with dancing, drumming, and song. Many villages hold colorful dances and masquerades, or masked dance-dramas. The traditional Christmas masquerade is the Ekon play. Dancers go from one family compound to another, where they present a doll representing the baby Jesus. Residents give gifts to the dancers before returning the doll.

Easter is also a national holiday, lasting from the Friday before Easter Sunday through the Monday after. Good Friday, commemorating Jesus's death, is a somber day of fasting and church services. Easter Sunday, celebrating Jesus's resurrection, or rising, from the dead, is a joyous occasion. People celebrate with feasting, dancing, drumming, and picnicking.

Religious Conflicts

Nigeria's religious diversity has an unfortunate aspect: religious conflict. The constitution provides for freedom of religion, and state and local governments are prohibited from endorsing an official religion. However, when northern states adopted shari'a law, the Christian minority saw this as an official government sponsorship of Islam.

The move created an atmosphere of tension between Christians and Muslims. As *dhimmis*, or non-Muslim minorities, northern Christians often face discrimination, harassment, and unreasonable imprisonment. Tensions have led to violence.

Traditional Beliefs

Traditional religions have ancient roots in Nigeria. Many groups recognize one supreme god. That god is Olorun or Olodumare among the Yoruba, Chukwu for the Igbo, Osalobua to the Edo, and Abasi Ibom among the Ibibio. Other groups honor an array of spirits. Ancestor spirits, honored in home shrines, are important in most family households. Witches have the power to bring either good or bad fortune. Witch doctors provide protection with medicines, charms, and rituals to drive out evil.

In Yoruba traditional religion, there are many variations of the creation story. One holds that Olorun sent his son, Oduduwa, to create the earth. Oduduwa descended from heaven on a chain to Ife, carrying a pigeon, a rooster, and a calabash (gourd) full of soil. After casting the soil across the waters, he set the rooster and the pigeon upon the soil. They scratched in the dirt, spreading dry land across the earth. Oduduwa is also identified as the first of the Yoruba kings. His 16 sons then founded the original Yoruba kingdoms. All subsequent Yoruba kings trace their ancestry back to Oduduwa.

The Osun-Osogbo Sacred Grove

On the outskirts of the city of Osogbo, alongside the Osun River, is a dense forest known as the Osun-Osogbo Sacred Grove. It is said to be the home of Osun, the Yoruba goddess of fertility. The area is filled with sculptures and images of Osun and other gods.

During an August festival, people dressed in white robes gather at the grove to renew the bonds between Osun and the people of Osogbo, who represent all of humanity. Sacred groves once surrounded all Yoruba settlements, but this may be the only one remaining.

One king, known as the Ooni of Ife, is the spiritual leader of the Yoruba.

The Yoruba honor hundreds of *orisha*, or secondary deities—gods and goddesses—with both male and female priests acting as intermediaries. During religious rituals, the orisha may take possession of a priest, who falls into a deep trance and takes on the character of the orisha. One orisha is Ogun, the god of war, the hunt, metalworking, and all who use metal tools in their work. The orisha Shango is the god of thunder and lightning. The Yoruba perform the lavish Gelede masquerade to honor the great mothers—their female elders, ancestors, and deities—and appeal to them for good fortune.

Yoruba ritual bowl

Among the Igbo, Ala is the earth goddess who oversees human morality and fertility. An array of minor gods and goddesses can bring blessings or harm. If someone suffers unexplained illness or continuous misfortune, he or she might consult a diviner, a type of priest who determines which deity has been offended. Then, offerings are made to make amends and set things right again. Various deities are represented by carved statues and by masks in masquerades. The spirits of ancestors are powerful beings, too. At meetings and social gatherings, people call on these spirits as they break kola nuts to share.

The Ijaw of the Niger Delta region also honor ancestor spirits, whom they represent in carved wooden figures. Because the Ijaw traditionally live by fishing, many of their religious practices center around *owuamapu*, or water spirits, that inhabit the rivers and swamps. Humans dwell among the water spirits before they are born and return there when they die. Elaborate funerals are held to assure safe passage back to the water spirit world. People appeal to the water spirits' goodwill in annual masquerades, where dancers wear masks in the forms of hippopotamuses, crocodiles, or fish.

Shrines honoring ancestors are important in the faith of the Ibibio people.

For the Ibibio, the major religious practices center on village ancestors. Heads of households and other prominent figures are the most important ancestors, and people make offerings to them at household shrines. Ancestors control their descendants' destinies and punish those who do not make proper offerings or who commit some offense. Offenders are called to task by members of the Ekpe (Egbo) society. This is a secret society of high-ranking men considered to be messengers of the ancestors. They act as a sort of moral law enforcement agency. Wearing masks, they confront the offender and perform ceremonies to appease the ancestors.

There are almost as many traditional beliefs and practices among Nigerians as there are ethnic groups. Although many Nigerians have adopted Christianity or Islam, their ancestral traditions continue to influence their approach to life.

Arts and Culture

ANDER THROUGH THE NIGERIAN COUNTRYSIDE, and you will hear music. Nigerians sing and dance to celebrate weddings and funerals, accompany festivals, welcome visitors, name babies, celebrate harvests, honor rulers, or tell stories. Or they may sing rhythmic work songs to accompany their daily chores. Men sing as they work their fields or row their canoes, and women sing as they prepare foods. Many songs follow the call-and-response structure, with a lead singer calling out a line and other singers repeating it or responding. Nigerians sing energetically and joyfully, often keeping the beat by swaying, dancing, clapping their hands, shaking rattles, or drumming.

Opposite: **Musicians play on the streets of Abuja.**

A Nigerian musician plays a traditional wind instrument.

Music, Dance, and Drama

Each of Nigeria's ethnic groups has its own music traditions. Hausa instruments include the *goje*, a single-stringed fiddle; the *kukkuma*, a small fiddle; the *kontigi*, a single-stringed lute; the *kakakai*, a trumpet 10 feet (3 m) or more long; and the talking drum, an hourglass-shaped drum whose pitch can be raised or lowered.

Arts and Culture **105**

It's called a talking drum because the changing pitches mimic the various tones of the people's spoken language.

Igbo musicians play the *obo*, a 13-stringed rectangular instrument; the *ekwe* and the *ufie*, which are slit drums, or wooden drums cut with an H-shaped slit; the *igba*, or cylinder drum; the *udu*, a pottery jug with a hole in the side; the *ogene* (metal gongs); and the *oja* (a flute), as well as wooden blocks, xylophones, and lyres.

Drumming is a well-developed art among the Yoruba. They call their talking drum the *dundun*, and *dundun* is also the name for a type of music that includes many kinds of drums. Other traditional Yoruba instruments include the *agogô* (bell), the *sekere* (gourd rattle), and the *agidigbo* (thumb piano). The thumb piano is a wooden board with thin metal strips of

Nigerian musicians play a tune with lutes, drums, and other traditional instruments.

different lengths attached. It's a popular instrument for children as well as adults. Players hold the board in both hands and pluck out melodies on the metal strips with their thumbs.

Music, dance, and drama are often combined. For example, during the Yoruba Gelede festival, dancers appear at midnight wearing enormous masks. Following the rhythm of beating drums, they perform a stomping dance to honor the earth, sing the praises of village elders, and relate comic tales about happenings in the community. The Ubakala Igbo use a dance-drama called *nkwa* to express their values or help settle conflicts. In the Girinya dance of the Tiv, men act out the motions of battle accompanied by wooden gongs and flutes.

The Ijaw of the Niger Delta hold an annual festival in honor of the mythical hero Ozidi. It features a weeklong performance of episodes in the life of Ozidi through song, dance, and other rituals. Traditional stories and legends are often the subjects of Nigerian folk opera. This art form involves elaborate costumes, swirling dances, vigorous drumming, and lively dialogue and chants. Other performances throughout the country include traveling puppet shows, masquerades, acrobatic acts, and dance-dramas.

A participant in the Gelede festival wears an elaborate mask with puppets on the top.

King Sunny Ade has been recording rich, dense dance music since the 1960s. He has been an international star since the late 1970s.

Nigerian popular music fuses traditional music with styles from around the world. Highlife became a popular style in the 1920s. It features jazz horns and several guitars. Another popular style, *juju*, is dance music that uses the talking drum, guitars, and shakers. Juju music is a specialty among the Yoruba of southwestern Nigeria. Musicians I. K. Dairo, Ebenezer Obey, and King Sunny Ade introduced juju to international audiences.

Yoruban Muslims developed *apala* music in the 1930s as a way to alert the faithful to the end of Ramadan fasting. Musicians play apala using rattles, thumb pianos, bells, and talking drums. Singer and musician Haruna Ishola made apala popular in the 1950s. His son, Musiliu Haruna Ishola, popularized apala with a new generation. *Were* music, performed in groups, also began as a Yoruban tradition during Ramadan. A modernized version entered the mainstream when Sikiru Ayinde Barrister added tambourine drums to create *fuji* music in the 1980s.

Musician Fela Kuti developed an energetic style of music called Afrobeat, combining Yoruba, highlife, jazz, and funk rock with call-and-response vocals. Popular singer Salawa

Abeni is known as the Queen of Waka Music, another Muslim-influenced Yoruban style. It's performed only by women, with melodic chants accompanied by rhythmic drums and rattles. Fans around the world enjoy the smooth style of singing star Sade. Born in Ibadan as Helen Folasade Adu, she is the lead singer in the British soft rock group Sade. Nigerian versions of gospel, reggae, and hip-hop are some of the many other styles that have emerged on the country's popular music scene.

Nigerian singer Sade captivates audiences with her smooth, haunting voice.

Playwrights and Novelists

Traditionally, Nigerians have passed on stories by word of mouth. Storytellers, elders, and parents recited time-honored folktales, proverbs, and chants. Beginning in the 20th century, many exceptional playwrights, poets, and novelists emerged.

Playwright Hubert Ogunde is honored as the father of Nigerian theater. He founded the Ogunde Concert Party, Nigeria's first professional theater company, in 1945. Aiming to revive an interest in traditional culture, he led the way in nurturing Nigerian folk opera, which features traditional music and dance.

Playwright Duro Ladipo is best known for *Oba kò so* (*The King Did Not Hang*, 1963), written in Yoruba. This classic Nigerian folk opera is based on a 500-year-old drama about the Yoruba religious figure Shango. Another playwright, Ola Rotimi, highlighted Nigeria's cultural diversity, often incorporating mime, dance, and traditional rituals into his plays. Playwright Wole Soyinka is a world-class writer who won the Nobel Prize in Literature in 1986.

Pita Nwana's 1933 book *Omenuko* was the first Igbo-language novel. Now a classic in Nigerian literature, it recounts the real-life travels and struggles of an Igbo man. Daniel Olorunfemi "D.O." Fagunwa was a Yoruba chief whose stories use the fantastic imagery of Yoruba folklore, such as spirits, monsters, gods, and magic. His 1938 novel *Ogboju Ode Ninu Igbo Irunmale* (*The Forest of a Thousand Demons*) was the first novel written in the Yoruba language.

Wole Soyinka: Poet and Playwright

Akinwande Oluwole "Wole" Soyinka (1934–) was born into a Yoruba family in Isara-Remo, Ogun State. After receiving a degree in English literature from England's University of Leeds, he returned to Nigeria and founded a theater company. His play *A Dance of the Forests* (1960) became the official play of Nigeria's independence. It uses satire to criticize romantic views of Nigeria's past. An outspoken activist, Soyinka was imprisoned for trying to arrange a peace agreement in 1967 during the Nigerian Civil War. While in prison, he wrote poetry that was published as *Poems from Prison*. He continued to write plays, poems, novels, and essays after his release, often criticizing the corrupt government. In 1986, he became the first black African to win the Nobel Prize in Literature. In 1997, Soyinka was charged with treason for criticizing dictator Sani Abacha, and since then he has spent much of his time in the United States.

Chimamanda Ngozi Adichie: "I Have to Write"

Novelist Chimamanda Ngozi Adichie (1977–) was born in Enugu to Igbo parents and grew up in Nsukka, where her father was a professor at the University of Nigeria. At age 19, she moved to the United States to attend college. Adichie's first novel, *Purple Hibiscus*, recounts the struggles of a Nigerian teenager and her family. It won the 2005 Commonwealth Writers' Prize for Best First Book. Her novel *Half of a Yellow Sun* received the 2007 Orange Prize for Fiction, a British award given to outstanding women writers. "I just write. I have to write," Adichie says. "I sometimes feel as if my writing is something bigger than I am."

The Igbo novelist Chinua Achebe portrays the clash between traditional Nigerian culture and Western values. His 1959 novel *Things Fall Apart* depicts the devastating effects of missionaries and colonists on Igbo life. This widely read book has been translated into about 50 languages. Flora Nwapa's *Efuru* (1966) was one of the first English-language novels by an African woman. Like her other novels, it depicts traditional Igbo life through a woman's eyes. The works of Chimamanda Ngozi Adichie focus on both political and cultural struggles. Her novel *Half of a Yellow Sun* follows three characters caught up in the civil war of the 1960s.

Arts and Crafts

The Nok people of central Nigeria were making terra-cotta statues as early as 500 BCE. These are Africa's earliest known sculptures. Other early Nigerian artworks are the terra-cotta heads of Ife and the bronze heads, statues, plaques, and animal

figures of Benin City, dating from about 1200 CE. Today, Nigerian folk arts range from mask carvings to body decorations.

Many people carve figures of ancestors, village heroes, or gods for household shrines. The Hausa are known for their gold and silver jewelry, ironwork, pottery, weaving, embroidery, and leather saddles, bags, and knife sheaths. The Fulani and other groups specialize in carving decorative patterns on calabashes.

This bronze Benin head dates back to the 16th century.

Some cultures also make ornate ceremonial masks. Igbo *ijele* masks, to honor the dead, are sometimes 12 feet (3.5 m) high. They show everyday scenes on several platforms built one above the other. Other Igbo masks accompany festivals, such as the masks for harvesttime

The Indigo Dye Pits of Kano

Each man squats beside a circular pit, soaking cotton cloth in bluish purple water. The men are skilled dyers at Kano's Kofar Mata dye pits, founded in 1498. The water is colored with indigo dye made from the leaves of the local indigo plant. Using centuries-old techniques, the dyers repeatedly dip the cloth, wring it out, and dry it in the open air. They then beat the dyed cloth to give it a shiny glaze. In centuries past, indigo textiles from Kano traveled the trade routes as far north as the Mediterranean Sea. Emirs preferred Kano's indigo cloth for their royal robes, and the Tuareg people of North Africa still use it for their robes, turbans, and veils.

The National Museum

Nigeria's National Museum has branches in Lagos, Jos, Kaduna, and Benin City. Each one features a variety of artistic and cultural exhibits. The National Museum in Jos displays a large collection of Nok terra-cotta heads and other figures. Its Pottery Hall features finely crafted pottery from all over the country. Other traditional handicrafts on display are masks, headdresses, and woodcarvings.

masquerades. Members of the Ekpe secret society of the Ibibio make black masks with movable jaws for their masquerades to assure health and maintain order in the village. The Ijo fishermen of the Niger Delta carve masks of water spirits in the form of crocodiles and hippopotamuses. Ekoi people make large masks that are covered with animal skins and have two or three faces, metal teeth, and inlaid stone or metal eyes.

Some groups adorn their bodies through scarification, or cutting scars. Scars are made in a young Ga'anda woman's forehead when she is engaged to be married. For the Tiv, scarification is considered necessary for a person to be beautiful. The Yoruba make facial and bodily scars to affirm their tribal identity and make themselves attractive. Scarification is becoming less common.

The Oshogbo Art Movement began in the 1950s in the Yoruba town of Oshogbo. Its artists aimed to use traditional themes in modern media such as paintings, woodcuts, bead paintings, batiks, appliqués, and metalwork. One of

This painting by Prince Twins Seven-Seven is entitled _Healing of Abiku Children._

the most prominent Oshogbo artists is Prince Twins Seven-Seven, who was born Prince Taiwo Olaniyi Wyewale-Toyeje Oyelale Osuntoki. His colorful artwork reflects Yoruba traditions and legends.

Uli designs are classic Igbo designs drawn with stark, simple lines. They may be geometric patterns, plants, animals, or stars. In the 1960s, artists at the University of Nigeria at Nsukka formed an association to revive this Igbo art by incorporating uli into modern works. Artist Chike Aniakor bases his ink and watercolor designs on uli figures. Intimately connected with Nigerian tradition, he says, "My painting ideas . . . mature with time like the sprouts of yam seedlings."

Sports

When it comes to team sports, Nigerians are wild about football, known in the United States as soccer. Schoolkids play on school soccer teams, and any group of kids is likely to start up an informal game in the street or on an open lot. Nigeria's national soccer team, the Super Eagles, is one of the best in Africa. They played in the World Cup in 1994, 1998, and 2002. The World Cup, the world's premier international soccer tournament, takes place every four years. The Eagles also won the African Cup of Nations in 1980 and 1994 and the gold medal in soccer at the 1996 Olympics in Atlanta, Georgia. The national women's soccer team has played in the Women's World Cup several times, too.

Nigerian athletes have had international success in track and field, basketball, and boxing. At the 1996 Summer Olympics, Chioma Ajunwa won the women's long-jump competition, becoming the first Nigerian to win an Olympic gold medal in an individual event. She is also the first African woman to win Olympic gold in a track-and-field event. Hakeem Olajuwon, who was born in Lagos, became a superstar in the National Basketball Association in the United States. The 7-foot (2.1 m) Yoruba athlete played center with the Houston Rockets and the Toronto Raptors, retiring in 2002. Nigerian boxer Samuel Peter, nicknamed the Nigerian Nightmare, became the World Boxing Council's heavyweight champion in 2008.

Nwankwo Kanu: Super Eagles Superstar

Nwankwo Kanu (1976–) is a superstar of Nigerian soccer. Born in Oweri to an Igbo family, Kanu has won more medals than any other African soccer player in history. Among his many honors are a Union of European Football Associations Cup medal, three Football Association Challenge Cup medals, and two African Player of the Year awards. Kanu, who is nicknamed Papilo, joined the Nigerian national team, the Super Eagles, in 1994. He became its captain in 2006, the same year he joined England's Portsmouth Football Club.

Kanu survived heart surgery in 1996, and he set up the Kanu Heart Foundation to help African children with heart defects. Kanu also works to help Nigerian children as a United Nations Children's Fund (UNICEF) Goodwill Ambassador.

Scenes of Daily Life

OLORFULLY DRESSED women pass by with goods stacked high on their heads, gliding along with a graceful sense of balance. They are a common sight in rural Nigeria, especially on market day. Market day is a grand affair for everyone, adults and children alike. The weekly market takes place in a central town on a certain day each week. People load up their goods and travel to market, sometimes on foot.

The market is laid out in the town square, where some people display their goods on the ground while others sell from stalls. They offer a dazzling array of wares— vegetables, fruit, firewood, spices, sandals, ready-to-eat snacks, pots and bowls, bags of water, jewelry, batteries, and goats. At the end of the day, buyers and sellers pack up and trek back to their villages.

Many Nigerian women learn to carry containers on their heads.

Opposite: **Workers unload crates of bananas at a fruit market in Kano.**

Village Life

About half of all Nigerians live in rural areas. For many, village life has changed little over the centuries. Villagers grow crops and raise livestock for a living. They pull up buckets of water by rope from an open well, use a hand pump to pump the water and fill containers, or carry water from a nearby river. Women cook meals over a wood-burning fire, either in the home or out in the open. Tending cattle is a man's job, although groups vary as to whether men, women, or both tend the fields and engage in trade. Children learn adult skills by helping parents with their daily chores.

A woman pumps water from a well. Hand-pump wells are the most common source of clean water in Nigeria.

Thatched roofs top circular homes in central Nigeria.

In rural areas, people live in settlements consisting of a cluster of homes. These groupings are family compounds, made up of many related people. Often they surround a central courtyard, where people socialize and children play. Some houses are built of dried mud, which keeps them cool in the hot climate. Other houses are built with wooden branches or woven straw. Roofs are thatch (layered straw) or corrugated metal. Several family compounds make up a village. In many places, an older, well-respected man is the village chief.

Naming Ceremonies

Children are treasured in Nigeria, and different ethnic groups hold different baby-naming ceremonies. Parents do not always choose the baby's name in advance. Rather, priests or elder relatives often designate favorable names for the child. The Yoruba naming ceremony takes place when the infant is eight days old.

Ceremonial foods are laid out, each with a symbolic meaning. An elder or a priest gives the baby a taste of each food and whispers the baby's names in its ear. Then a poet sings a specially written poem to express joy at the child's arrival. Finally, guests enjoy a big feast, complete with music and dancing.

Shoppers and vendors crowd a market in Lagos.

City Scenes

Life in the cities is more crowded and fast-paced than in rural villages. Streets are full of cars, trucks, buses, and taxis that whiz by at high speeds. Motorbikes weave in and out of traffic, zooming around any obstacles. Street traders hawk their wares, selling clothes, fruit, bread, newspapers, or phone cards. Pedestrians hurry on their way to markets, mosques, and offices.

Large cities such as Lagos and Abuja have elegant business districts where streets are lined with office buildings, restaurants, travel agencies, and banks. In the cities, poor people crowd into shacks. Middle-class residents live in modern houses or apartment buildings, while very wealthy people live in grand mansions surrounded by fences or walls. Muslim cities such as Kano feature a centuries-old,

Nigeria's Public Holidays

New Year's Day	January 1
Easter	March or April
Workers' Day	May 1
Democracy Day	May 29
Independence Day	October 1
Christmas	December 25–26

Three Muslim events are also national holidays. Their dates change from year to year.

Mouloud (birth of the Prophet)

'Id al-Fitr (end of Ramadan)

'Id al-Kabir (Feast of the Sacrifice)

mud-wall style of architecture. A large family compound consists of many rooms surrounding an indoor courtyard. Certain rooms are only for men, while others are reserved for women and children.

Clothing, Traditional and Modern

In Nigeria's cities, some residents dress the same as people in Western countries, and others wear traditional Nigerian clothing. Traditional clothes are more common as business attire in the north, while Western clothing is more common in the south. For cultural or ceremonial events, people wear traditional outfits. Young people wear both colorful traditional attire and casual Western clothes such as T-shirts and baseball caps.

Each ethnic group has its own style of dress. In general, women wear either a long, one-piece dress or a loose, long-sleeved blouse with a wrapped cloth skirt. They may wear a headcloth in many styles—tied as a scarf, folded, gathered in the back, or wound around like a turban. Some wear a long shawl-like scarf around the neck or tied diagonally across the body.

In many parts of Nigeria, traditional clothes are common.

Traditional clothing for men consists of a loose shirt that reaches to mid-thigh and loose-fitting trousers. On special occasions, men wear a V-necked robe with long, loose sleeves over their other clothing. Their head covering is a round cap or the white knit cap or embroidered cap of Muslim men in the north. Many Hausa men wear a long, flowing robe and a colored turban. White is a symbol of piety for Muslims, so Muslim men wear white clothing for religious events. Religious leaders in the north usually wear white robes and a white turban.

Loose robes and turbans help protect Nigerian men from the hot sun.

Foods and Beverages

Nigerian food is hot and spicy, with lots of peppers. Foods may be flavored with garlic, onion, or gingerroot and peppery spices made by grinding up seeds such as *atariko*, *uda*, and *gbafilo*. In much of Nigeria, the major foods are yams, rice, beans, corn, cassava root, and plan-tains, a type of banana. Many foods are cooked in palm oil or peanut oil and spiced with hot chili peppers.

Beef with papayas and rice is a traditional Christmas meal in Nigeria.

Yams may be cut up and boiled or fried. To make *iyan*, or pounded yam, the yams are boiled in water, ending up thick and smooth like mashed potatoes. *Amala* is a similar yam paste. These dishes are eaten with soups or stews such as *ewedu* (boiled green leaves) or *ila* (boiled okra).

Many dishes consist only of vegetables, but meats such as beef, chicken, lamb, goat, or fish are often added to soups. *Obe ata*, or pepper soup, is a thick sauce made of tomatoes, ground pepper, meat or fish, onions, vegetable or palm oil, and spices. *Egusi* soup is a stew of meat or fish and vegetables, thickened with ground melon seeds. *Suya* makes a spicy meat snack. It's made of spiced meat and vegetables grilled on a stick.

Gari is cassava root that has been ground, soaked, and strained. It can be boiled and rolled into balls called *fufu* for scooping up sauce or stew. Or it can be mixed with water

Goat meat is a common ingredient in many Nigerian dishes.

or milk and eaten as a snack. Corn has many preparations, too. It can be roasted or boiled on the cob, or the kernels can be boiled with beans to make *adalu*. For *aadun*, the corn is ground, mixed with red pepper and oil, wrapped in ewe leaves, and baked. It makes a spicy snack.

Jollof rice can be an entire meal or just one dish at a big feast. It's a mixture of rice with tomatoes, onions, and spices that have been fried in peanut oil. Meat and other vegetables can be added to create unique flavors.

In the north, many foods are made with grains such as millet, corn, sorghum, and rice. The grains are ground into flour to make various foods. A favorite northern dish is *tuwo da miya*, a thick sorghum stew eaten with a spicy sauce of tomatoes, onions, and peppers. Peanuts, cowpeas, sweet potatoes, and other root foods are also common in the north. Muslims do not eat pork, as Islam forbids it. However, they eat beef or goat meat, served either in sauces or as kabobs (*tsire*).

What's for Breakfast?

For the Yoruba, *ogi* is a popular breakfast food. It's dried and powdered corn that's boiled into a smooth porridge. People often eat ogi with a ground-up mixture of beans, tomatoes, and peppers, served as a steamed version (*moyin-moyin*) or a fried (*akara*) version. *Gari* (from cassava) is a common breakfast food, too. It's sprinkled with sugar and eaten like cereal.

Some people enjoy fried plantains (*dodo*) for breakfast. Others eat rice, mangoes, or stewed soybeans. A Hausa breakfast might be cakes made of ground, fried beans (*kosai*) or fried wheat-flour cakes served with sugar (*funkaso*). In areas near the sea, people may enjoy a breakfast of fish or crab stew mixed with cassava. These all make hearty meals to begin the day.

Breaking the Kola Nut

In much of Nigeria, especially among the Igbo, kola nuts are both a food and a ceremonial symbol. These reddish seeds, about 2 inches (5 cm) long, grow inside pods on the kola nut tree. Kola nuts are presented to guests to welcome them as they enter a home. The nuts are broken into sections and passed around, and the host or senior guest takes the first bite. This gesture is a way of offering peace, friendship, and hospitality. Kola nuts are also offered to chiefs as a sign of reverence. An important meeting may begin with a kola nut ceremony. This assures that the proceedings will take place in peace and harmony.

Common beverages include tea, soft drinks, local fruit juices, and bottled water. Maltina, produced locally, is a sweet malt drink. Some people like to mix it with coffee. A drink called *zobo* originated among the Hausa of northern Nigeria and spread to other regions. It's made of juice from the leaves of the roselle plant, with sugar and fruit flavorings added. Zobo is believed to have medicinal value.

Hot tea is a popular drink in Nigeria.

Children's Games

In the cities, children in middle- and upper-class homes play computer games. In rural villages, children enjoy traditional games. Many pass the time with call-and-response singing games, often using ancient versions of their language. They might play instruments they make from cornstalks and drums they make with tin cans.

Igbo girls play *oga*, with one or more girls facing the leader. They begin singing a song and dancing, and at a hand clap, they stop with their legs in a certain position. If one player's leg position matches the leader's, she gets to be the leader next. Igbo boys play *ogu obogwu* (duck fight). Two boys face each other squatting. They jump up and down, spreading their arms and legs and swatting at each other. The first one to fall onto his backside is the loser.

Some children enjoy playing a board game called *ayo*. Other games involve running, chasing, or jumping. To play "jumping the beanbag," one player takes a rope with a sack

Let's Play Ayo!

Yoruba children and adults enjoy a board game called *ayo*. People make wooden ayo boards with 12 small cuplike depressions arranged in two rows. At each end is a large cup used as a bank for each of the two players. At the beginning, each small cup has four seeds or pebbles, and the large cups contain six each. The first player takes all the seeds from one of the small cups and places one seed in each of the next cups, going in a counterclockwise direction. If the last seed lands in a cup on the opponent's side, the player takes all those seeds and adds them to his or her bank. The game ends when a player cannot make a move. Then, the one with the most seeds in the bank is the winner.

This game is popular in many regions of Africa. In Egypt, where the game originated, it is called mancala. It is *okwe* to the Igbo, *darra* among the Hausa, and *iyagbe* for the Edo.

Schoolchildren in Abuja play a clapping game.

tied to the end and swings it around in a circle on the ground as the other players jump over the sack. Any player hit by the sack is out. The last person left gets to swing the sack next. In "catch your tail," two teams join hands, forming two chains. The two people on the end of each chain wear a "tail"—a scarf or handkerchief in their pocket or belt. The two chains chase each other, trying to snatch the other's tail.

Happy People

Although many Nigerians suffer economic difficulties, their culture provides a deep source of satisfaction. In 2003, the World Values Survey of more than 65 countries found that Nigeria had the highest percentage of happy people in the world. Some Nigerians say their family life is what makes them happy. Some say it is their music. Others derive happiness from their faith and their values. "We have a great religious faith," explains one villager. "We all believe ardently that God is looking after us. We believe in being our brother's keeper."

Timeline

Nigerian History		World History	
		c. 3000 BCE	Forms of writing are invented in China, India, and Sumeria.
		c. 2500 BCE	Egyptians build pyramids in Giza.
		c. 563 BCE	The Buddha is born in India.
The Nok civilization thrives in the Jos Plateau region.	500 BCE–200 CE	c. 469 BCE	Socrates is born in Greece.
		313 CE	Roman emperor Constantine recognizes Christianity.
		610	The Prophet Muhammad begins preaching Islam.
		618–907	The Tang Dynasty rules China.
Igbo leader Ìfikuánim becomes the first ruler of Nri.	1043 CE		
Hausa states are established in northern Nigeria.	c. 1100		
The Yoruba Kingdom unites.	1100s		
		1206–1227	Genghis Khan rules the Mongol Empire.
		1215	King John of England agrees to the Magna Carta.
		1300s	The Renaissance begins in Italy.
The Yoruba Kingdom moves north to Oyo.	1400s	1400s	The Inca flourish in the Andes, and the Aztec thrive in what is now Mexico.
The Edo kingdom of Benin flourishes.	1400s–1500s	1464	The Songhay Empire is established in West Africa.
Portuguese trading ships arrive on the southern coast.	1472	1492	Christopher Columbus arrives in the Americas.
		1502	Enslaved Africans are first brought to the Americas.
		1517	The Protestant Reformation begins.
Great Britain has a monopoly on the European slave trade in Nigeria.	1700s	1776	Americans sign the Declaration of Independence.

Nigerian History

Fulani leader Usman dan Fodio founds the Sokoto Caliphate in northern Nigeria.	1804
Great Britain outlaws the slave trade in Nigeria and other lands under British control.	1807
Great Britain forms the Colony and Protectorate of Nigeria.	1914
Herbert Macaulay founds Nigeria's first political party, the Nigerian National Democratic Party.	1923
Igbo leader Nnamdi Azikiwe founds the pro-independence newspaper *West African Pilot*.	1937
Nigeria declares independence from Great Britain.	1960
Military officers overthrow the prime minister in a coup in January; a second coup follows in July.	1966
Southeastern provinces secede, leading to the Nigerian Civil War, or Biafran War.	1967–1970
Nigeria becomes one of the world's largest producers of oil.	1970s
A drop in world oil prices plunges Nigeria into an economic collapse.	1982
Olusegun Obasanjo becomes Nigeria's first civilian president in 16 years.	1999
The Movement for the Emancipation of the Niger Delta emerges, in militant opposition to the oil industry in the delta.	2006
Umaru Yar'Adua is elected president in Nigeria's first transition from one civilian leader to another.	2007

World History

1804	Haiti becomes independent following the only successful slave uprising in history.
1823	The United States announces the Monroe Doctrine.
1861–1865	American Civil War
1914–1918	World War I
1917	The Bolshevik Revolution brings communism to Russia.
1929	A worldwide economic depression sets in.
1939–1945	World War II
1950s–1960s	African colonies win independence from European nations.
1957–1975	Vietnam War
1989	The cold war ends as communism crumbles in Eastern Europe.
1994	South Africa abolishes apartheid.
2001	Terrorists attack the World Trade Center in New York City and the Pentagon in Arlington, Virginia.
2004	A tsunami in the Indian Ocean destroys coastlines in Africa, India, and Southeast Asia.
2008	The United States elects its first African American president.

Fast Facts

Official name: Federal Republic of Nigeria

Capital: Abuja

Official language: English

Major ethnic groups: Hausa-Fulani, Yoruba, Igbo (Ibo), Ijaw, Kanuri, Ibibio, Tiv

Abuja

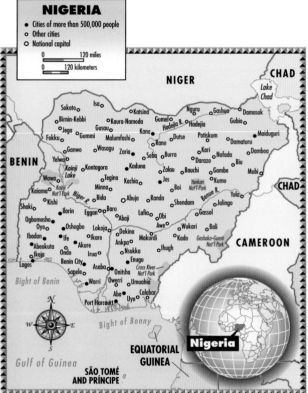

Nigeria's flag

Yam field

Year of independence:	1960
National anthem:	"Arise, O Compatriots"
Form of government:	Federal republic
Head of state:	President
Head of government:	President
Area:	356,669 square miles (923,768 sq km)
Greatest distance north to south:	About 650 miles (1,045 km)
Greatest distance east to west:	About 750 miles (1,200 km)
Latitude and longitude of geographic center:	10°N, 8°E
Borders:	Niger to the north, Chad to the northeast, Cameroon to the east, Benin to the west
Highest elevation:	Chappal Waddi, 7,936 feet (2,419 m) above sea level
Lowest elevation:	Sea level, along the Atlantic Ocean
Average high temperatures:	In Lagos, 90°F (32°C) in March and 82°F (28°C) in September; in Kano, 99°F (37°C) in March and 88°F (31°C) in September
Average low temperatures:	In Lagos, 79°F (26°C) in March and 55°F (13°C) in September; in Kano, 66°F (19°C) in March and 70°F (21°C) in September
Average annual rainfall:	In Lagos, 72 inches (183 cm); in Kano, 33 inches (84 cm)

Osun-Osogbo Sacred Grove

Length of coastline:	530 miles (853 km)	
Longest river:	Niger River	
National population (2006 census):	140,003,542	
Population of largest cities (2008 est.):	Lagos	9,494,045
	Ibadan	4,826,891
	Kano	2,330,412
	Benin City	2,238,589
	Kaduna	1,926,356

Landmarks:
- ▶ *Aso Rock,* Abuja
- ▶ *Central Mosque,* Abuja
- ▶ *Chief Ogiamen's House,* Benin City
- ▶ *Cocoa House,* Ibadan
- ▶ *Gidan Rumfa (Emir's Palace),* Kano
- ▶ *Osun-Osogbo Sacred Grove,* Osogbo

Economy: The oil industry is Nigeria's major industry, accounting for about 98 percent of the country's export earnings in 2006. Much of Nigeria's manufacturing activity centers around petroleum products. Other manufactured goods include cement, food products including wheat flour and palm oil, steel, tires, and assembled vehicles. Major agricultural products include cassava, yams, sorghum, cocoa, and rubber.

Currency: The naira. In April 2009, US$1.00 was equal to 147.2 naira.

System of weights and measures: Metric system

Currency

Schoolchildren

Wole Soyinka

Literacy rate (2006): Men, 73.0%

Women, 55.4%

**Common words
and phrases:**

English	Hausa	Yoruba	Igbo
Hello	*Sànnu*	*Ago o*	*Kelou or Kadu*
How are you?	*Kana lafiyà?*	*Bá wo ni?*	*Kedu ka odi?*
Fine, thanks	*Lafiyà lau*	*Dáadáa ni esa*	*O di mma*
Good-bye	*Sai an jimà*	*O da bo*	*Ka omesia*

Notable Nigerians: Muhammadu Sa'adu Abubakar (1956–)
Sultan of Sokoto

Chinua Achebe (1930–)
Novelist

Chimamanda Ngozi Adichie (1977–)
Novelist

Samuel (Ajayi) Crowther (c. 1809–1891)
First African Anglican bishop of Nigeria

Philip Emeagwali (1954–)
Scientist

Usman dan Fodio (1754–1817)
Founder of the Sokoto Caliphate

Fela Kuti (1938–1997)
Musician

Herbert Macaulay (1864–1946)
Politician

Hubert Ogunde (1916–1990)
Playwright and musician

Hakeem Olajuwon (1963–)
Basketball player

Sade (Helen Folasade Adu) (1959–)
Singer

Wole Soyinka (1934–)
Nobel Prize–winning poet and playwright

To Find Out More

Nonfiction

▶ Dell, Pamela. *Teens in Nigeria*. Minneapolis: Compass Point Books, 2008.

▶ Gordon, April. *Nigeria's Diverse Peoples: A Reference Sourcebook*. Santa Barbara, Calif.: ABC-CLIO, 2003.

▶ Harmon, Daniel E. *Nigeria, 1880 to the Present: The Struggle, the Tragedy, the Promise*. Philadelphia: Chelsea House, 2000.

▶ Koslow, Philip. *Lords of the Savanna: The Bambara, Fulani, Igbo, Mossi, and Nupe*. Philadelphia: Chelsea House, 1997.

▶ Nnoromele, Salome C. *Life Among the Ibo Women of Nigeria*. San Diego: Lucent Books, 1998.

▶ Onyefulu, Ifeoma. *One Big Family: Sharing Life in an African Village*. London, U.K.: Frances Lincoln Children's Books, 2006.

▶ Rosenberg, Anne. *Nigeria: The Culture*. New York: Crabtree, 2001.

Fiction

▶ McIntosh, Gavin. *Hausaland Tales from the Nigerian Marketplace*. North Haven, Conn.: Linnet Books, 2002.

▶ Ogumefu, M. I. *Yoruba Legends*. Sioux Falls, S.D.: NuVision Publications, 2007.

DVDs

▶ *Ancient Nok Art Culture of Nigeria*. CustomFlix, 2006.

▶ *Konkombe: The Nigerian Pop Music Scene*. Shanachie, 2000.

▶ *Obara and the Merchants*. Victory Multimedia, 2008.

Web Sites

▶ **Community Portal of Nigeria: Customs and Traditions**
www.onlinenigeria.com/
traditions_Customs.asp
To find out about the customs and traditions of Nigeria's diverse ethnic groups.

▶ **Motherland Nigeria: Kid Zone**
www.motherlandnigeria.com/
kidzone.html
To learn about Nigerian games, stories, schools, and much more.

▶ **Nigerian Tourism Development Corporation**
www.tourism.gov.ng
To find out about Nigeria's national parks, festivals, foods, and other attractions.

Embassies and Organizations

▶ **Embassy of the Federal Republic of Nigeria**
3519 International Court, NW
Washington, DC 20008
202-986-8400
www.nigeriaembassyusa.org

▶ **Nigeria High Commission, Ottawa, Canada**
295 Metcalfe Street
Ottawa, Ontario
K2P 1R9
Canada
613-236-0521
www.nigeriahcottawa.com

Index

Page numbers in *italics* indicate illustrations.

Meet the Author

ANN HEINRICHS fell in love with faraway places while reading Doctor Dolittle books as a child. Now, she tries to cover as much of the earth as possible. She has traveled through most of the United States and much of Europe, as well as the Middle East, East Asia, and Africa. She has traveled among the Hausa people of Niger, who share a culture with the people of northern Nigeria.

Heinrichs grew up roaming the woods of Arkansas. Now, she lives in Chicago. She is the author of more than 200 books for children and young adults on American, European, Asian, and African history and culture. Several of her books have won national and state awards.

"To me, writing nonfiction is a bigger challenge than writing fiction," Heinrichs says. "With nonfiction, you can't just dream something up—everything has to be true. Finding out facts is harder than making things up, but to me it's more rewarding. When I uncover the facts, they always turn out to be more spectacular than fiction could ever be. And I'm always on the lookout for what kids in another country are up to, so I can report back to kids here."

Heinrichs has also written numerous newspaper, magazine, and encyclopedia articles and has worked as a children's book editor and an advertising copywriter. She enjoys bicycling and kayaking and is an award-winning martial artist, specializing in t'ai chi empty-hand and sword forms.

Photo Credits